ANTHROPOLOGICAL METHODS FOR COMMUNICATION RESEARCH

About the Editor

Binod C. Agrawal (Ph.D. Anthropology, 1970, University of Wisconsin, Madison, USA) is a well-known International Communication Research expert. He has a reputation of being innovative in research methods and techniques, institution building, management and teaching leadership. Founder Director of several institutions and a university. Earlier he worked for over two decades and pioneered use of qualitative methods for communication research during the world famous Satellite Instructional Television Experiment (SITE), 1975-76 and led an interdisciplinary SITE social research team of over 100 social scientists. Author of two dozen books and several dozen articles in national and International Journals and continues to publish. He is currently the Mentor of Media Research Centre at School of Communication, Manipal Academy of Higher Education, Manipal.

ANTHROPOLOGICAL METHODS FOR COMMUNICATION RESEARCH

Experiences and Encounters During SITE

Edited by
BINOD C. AGRAWAL

Assisted by
SASHIKALA VISWANATH

CONCEPT PUBLISHING COMPANY PVT. LTD.
NEW DELHI-110059

ISBN : 978-81-7022-113-5

Edition 2022

Published and Printed by

Since 1974

Concept Publishing Company Pvt. Ltd.
A/15-16, Commercial Block, Mohan Garden,
New Delhi-110059 (INDIA)
T : +91 11 41101460
E : publishing@conceptpub.com, *W* : www.conceptpub.com

Cataloging in Publication Data--Courtesy: D.K. Agencies (P) Ltd. <docinfo@dkagencies.com>

Anthropological methods for communication research : experiences and encounters during SITE/ edited by Binod C. Agrawal ; assisted by Sashikala Viswanath.
pages cm
ISBN 9788170221135

1. Satellite Instructional Television Experiment (India). 2. Anthropology--Research--India. 3. Anthropology--India--Methodology. 4. Communication--India--Research. I. Agrawal, Binod C., 1942- editor. II. Viswanath, Sashikala, editor.

LCC HE8700.9.I5A58 2022 | DDC 302.20954 23

PREFACE

SATELLITE Instructional Television Experiment (SITE) was one of the most advanced and probably the largest experiment conducted on human communication. SITE was a pilot project which provided a new system of communication. It had certain objectives, namely that of providing information to the villagers and thereby inducing change and development. And sure enough, its impact was felt. SITE was one such experiment in which anthropologists were induced to conduct indepth qualitative, descriptive studies for understanding the process of communication. A group of young anthropologists having basic training in this discipline decided to accept the challenge and conduct a Holistic Study of traditional type, with fairly innovative objectives connected with high technology like Satellite Communication. In their diaries they wrote a detailed account of their field work and personal experiences. After the field work, each of the anthropologists were asked to write a short account describing their personal experiences in the field. The accounts were entitled "Hello to Goodbye"

The attempt in the present venture is to draw upon the methodological data pertaining to the life situations encountered, perceived and felt by the anthropologists and provide a perspective of anthropological and human dimensions of communication research. Participant observation was the major technique employed for the study.

Each of the authors, in their accounts broadly covered topics like—the initial entry into the village, problems faced in locating accommodations, description of their home, description of their interactions with the villagers, jati affiliation, the key informants and the means employed to locate the key informants, descriptions of their life style in pre-SITE, SITE, and post-SITE field work, their image created in the village, and finally their departure. While preparing individual accounts of the anthropologists, care has been taken to maintain the uniformity in documenting the individual field experiences of each anthropologist.

This book is divided into three parts. In the first part, the theoretical and methodological issues and instructions for anthropologists have been discussed. In the second part the personal experience of seven anthropologists have been narrated. In the last part, the field work manual has been provided. This book is an attempt to provide a perspective to anthropologists and communication researchers intending to initiate similar studies.

Chapter one 'Holistic Study : An Indepth Perspective' is a condensation from the paper published in *Media Asia—An Asian Mass Communication Quarterly*, Vol. 8, No. 3, Singapore : Amic Publication, 1981 pp : 139-146. Chapter two, 'Methodological Strategy for Communication Research, is taken from my book *Television Comes to Village : An Evaluation of SITE*, Bangalore : Indian Space Research Organisation, 1978 pp : 9-32. Chapter three 'In the Field' and Chapter eleven 'Instructions for Field Work' were prepared by J.K. Doshi, K.K. Verma and me, who were the project leaders for the study. Chapter three was further enriched with the help of Ms. Sashikala Viswanath who recast this Chapter to provide a perspective to researchers in the field. Chapter four to ten consist of the seven anthropologists' personal account.

All the field diaries were written in the language of the field area. However, anthropologists wrote "Hello to Goodbye" in English. These accounts were rewritten by Ms. Sashikala Viswanath (after a lapse of several years) without changing the content, form and the authors' native touch. Several discussions beween Ms Viswanath and myself took place before rewriting the original manuscript. All attempts during this process were made to keep the 'feeling tone' of the original work.

It was in late 1974, that K.K. Verma and J.K. Doshi joined me in the evaluative study of SITE. Both being anthropologists, they took keen interest in this research and the responsibility of the Holistic Study was shared by the three of us. Until they left this organization, we jointly conceived, planned and closely monitored this study. I am grateful to them for their assistance and co-operation.

Professor Yash Pal, the then Director, SAC, Ahmedabad, encouraged, discussed and participated in the Holistic Study workshops and made many valuable suggestions. I sincerely thank him for his help. Professor E.V. Chitnis, (now Director, SAC) contribution to this study goes beyond the professional role of SITE Programme Manager. I am grateful to him for his consistent support to my efforts.

I am thankful to the authors, J.B. Ambekar, M.N. Jha, K.K. Pandey, Kumkum Rai, Ravi P. Rai, M.V.T. Raju, and Arbind K. Sinha for doing excellent work and accepting hardships without complaint. Mrs Nalini Srinivasan worked very closely with me in Ahmedabad. I appreciate her assistance in monitoring and co-ordinating the field work. Just before SITE was over, Bageshwar Singh joined the project and assisted field anthropologists in the writing of the individual reports and closely participated in the project activities. I am sincerely grateful to him for his assistance.

In the Centre, my colleagues B.S. Bhatia, K.S. Karnik, Arup Das Gupta and N. Sampath not only helped in the planning of the study but also participated in the deliberations and made valuable suggestions. I am deeply indebted to them for their help.

This work would have remained unfinished without the help of Arbind K. Sinha, who even now continues to work with me. I take this opportunity to thank him.

This book was written with the assistance of Ms. Sashikala Viswanath, whose suggestions and ideas were immensely valuable. She assisted me in editing Chapters one, two and three. Without the enthusiasm of Sashi I would have been unable to clear the dusty pages, sit for hours together and check and verify some of the anthropologists accounts. Her imaginations for translating some of the accounts into readable sentences helped in completing this work. I am sincerely grateful to her for assisting me in editing this book.

Mr. K.K. Raghavan was the one who has been with me since I started on this project, hence it was possible with his ingenuity to keep every record intact. I am sincerely thankful to him for his assistance.

Ahmedabad
15 July 1984

BINOD C. AGRAWAL

LIST OF MAPS

CONTENTS

LIST OF PLATES

CHAPTER ONE

HOLISTIC STUDY : AN INDEPTH PERSPECTIVE

by

BINOD C. AGRAWAL

Binod C. Agrawal Ph.D. in Anthropology, worked as Project Leader during SITE. He continues to work at Space Applications Centre, Ahmedabad. He was born in a Hindi speaking family of Uttar Pradesh. He was educated in Hindi and English being the medium of instruction in school and college.

TV in the study village

HOLISTIC STUDY : AN INDEPTH PERSPECTIVE

—BINOD C. AGRAWAL

ANTHROPOLOGY AND COMMUNICATION

IN 1976, I attended my first non-anthropological meeting at the Open University, United Kingdom. I remember that it was an international conference on evaluation and research in educational television and radio. During the conference, participants from South America, Asia, North America and Europe gave suggestions about the utility of anthropological methods in media evaluation. While summarizing the various methods that were suggested for media research, McAnany (1977 : 357) included the anthropological methods in the list which have been closely identified with 'holistic' or 'illuminative' research.... In a small article, that I had submitted in the conference, the terms 'anthropology' and 'media research' appeared, to the best of my knowledge, for the first time in such a gathering. (Agrawal 1977a : 285-287).

In 1978, when the Xth International Congress of Anthropological and Ethnological Sciences met in India, I was pleasantly surprized to note that there were symposia focused on commu-

The field experiences of Dadusar could not be translated which was originally written in Gujarati. Both in Sakarra and Ghenupali three anthropologists conducted the whole field work, hence, it was omitted from the presentation.

nication and development. In 1979, East-West communication Institute in United States made special efforts to involve anthropologists in their communication research and evaluation in general and Indonesian Satellite TV evaluation project in particular. (Alfian and Chu 1979).

There are indications that in other schools of communication, there is a growing interest in the applications of anthropological knowledge in communication research and evaluation. I have chosen to use the term 'anthropological application' as I am concerned with the application of methods and techniques of anthropology to understand the process of information transfer from a medium to human beings. I have given this historical scenario to emphasize that there is a growing recognition about the usefulness of anthropological methods and techniques in communication research and evaluation. More so in Asian and African countries.

In India, anthropologists have been working in Audience Research Unit of All India Radio (AIR) for several years. These anthropologists tend to work like audience research officers rather than anthropologists. In the early seventies, when social evaluation plan for Satellite Instructional Television Experiment (SITE) was being drawn, among many studies, an idea was mooted to conduct 'holistic study'. Nothing was described or defined about 'holistic study'.

A seminar was organised in May 1973, to discuss the plan of action for social evaluation of Satellite Instructional Television Experiment (SITE). It was a meeting of social scientists from various disciplines. They suggested that qualitative descriptive evaluation, in addition to sample survey should be conducted to evaluate the effects of satellite TV on maiden rural viewers. The suggestion was based on their past experiences and growing dissatisfaction with the methodological inadequacies of sample survey in the context of rural India.

In the beginning of 1974, the role of anthropologists in the social evaluation of SITE was not even defined. It was left to the anthropologists to define their own role though there were tasks to be carried out on priority basis to fulfil the earlier commitments. These included 'audience profile' and 'need assessment study.' Therefore, the first job was to define the total task of research and evaluation related to SITE.

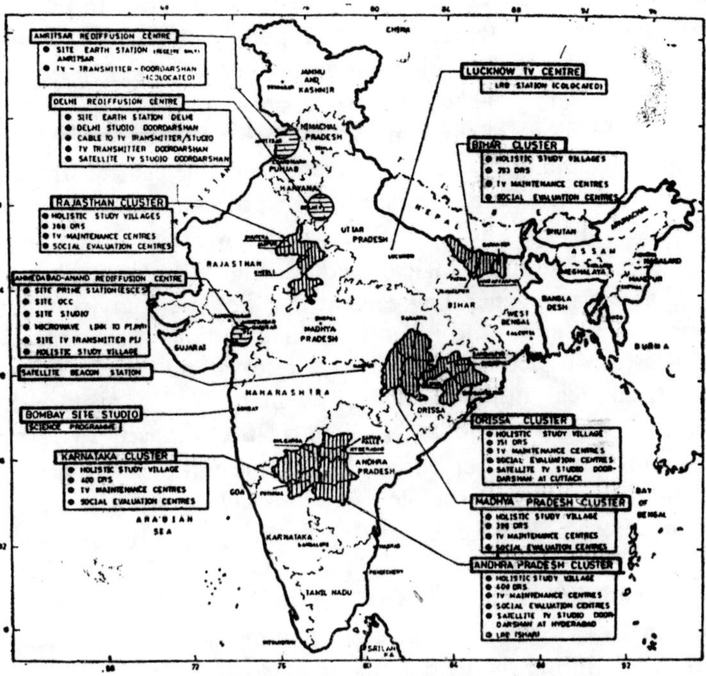

Map showing Holistic Study Centres

Almost after a year in May 1974, another seminar was held to finalize the SITE social evaluation plan in which a *draft plan* was discussed. The participants felt that "one could not live within the boundaries of their own disciplines while participating in a project like SITE . . . . In this way, the 'social evaluation plan' was conceived as *inter* disciplinary and *multi* disciplinary, involving many disciplines of social sciences" (Agrawal 1977b : 122). Five types of communication research and evaluation were suggested :

1. *Policy Evaluation*—goal determination and operationalization of the policy ;
2. *Context Evaluation*-(Pre-Production Research) ;
3. *Input Evaluation*—(Production Research) ;
4. *Process Evaluation*—(Telecast Research) ; and
5. *Summative Evaluation*—(Post-Telecast Research).

These five types were considered as integral to the total communication research and evaluation as indicated elsewhere (Agrawal 1976). In this seminar, each of the five types of evaluation were touched upon. As the policy evaluation was beyond the scope of the seminar, the other four types and especially the summative evaluation remained the central theme of the discussion. Context, input and process evaluations were discussed in which little concern was shown about the appropriateness of anthropological methods and techniques.

There was a general agreement that holistic study could provide a qualitative and indepth understanding of the effects of TV on rural viewers. However, reservations were expressed about the 'real' utility of such an evaluation in the future planning of Indian National Satellite (INSAT) based TV system. Even after it was accepted, a continuous battle was waged against holistic study by sociologists who saw very little utility of such an evaluation for answering planning questions which in their opinion required hard data. In this book an effort has been made to document, the theoretical, methodological and personal experiences of the anthropologists. The instructions prepared during the field study are also included.

Anthropological perspective in Communication Research and Evaluation

The distinct anthropological 'approach' or 'perspective' must be spelt out before describing the anthropologists involvement in SITE social research and evaluation especially in conducting summative evaluation.

The holistic view : "Anthropologists, contrary to other social scientists are interested in understanding all the manifestations of human beings and of human activity in a unified way, conceiving it as a whole' (Agrawal 1977a : 285). "Anthropology more than any other social or behavioural science, has resisted simplistic, reductionistic explanations of social phenomena. The holistic perspective encourages anthropologists, to consider a wide range of casual factors while attempting to understand human behaviour—biological, social, cultural, psychological, economic, political, ecological, and many others" (Olien 1978 : 14). "A fundamental proposition of anthropology is that no part can be fully or even accurately, understood apart from the whole"

(Hoebal 1966 : 4). Hence, it was considered essential that communication whether satellite or human being culture bound, must be studied while focusing human beings in their totality.

Process analysis : Fifty years ago Sapir observed that "every cultural pattern and every single act of social behaviour involves communication in either an explicit or implicit sense" (Sapir 1931 reprinted in Berelson and Janowitz 1966: 169). Schramm a communication expert thinks that "society is a sum of relationships in which information of some kind is shared. Let us understand clearly one thing about it : Human communication is *something people do*. It has no life of its own" (Schramm 1973 : 3).

Having a holistic view of human behaviour, anthropologists have tried to analyse the various parts, their internal inter-relations and interactions as a dynamic set of processes. Such an approach has helped anthropologists to avoid static ethnographic description of a culture. Applications of such a perspective would help analyse communication acts as a process in different social situations and role relationships.

Emic approach : Emic approach allows anthropologists to participate, observe and study the cultural categories in which a linguistic group, categorizes, classifies and interprets any new messages (Hariss 1968 : 570-572). As opposed to *emic* approach *etic* approach allows analysis of social phenomena in pre-determined and universally accepted categories. Both these terms have been adopted from linguistics. "The anthropologist is generally more sensitive to the problems posed by *emic/etic* differences than many other social scientists, and consequently the anthropologists have learned to appreciate the way of life of the society in its own terms. (Olien 1978 : 15).

Comparative perspective : Generally, anthropologists conduct their study in a single culture, in a small 'community'. Even in the village study, they tend to conduct their field work in a single village. Therefore, it is logical to raise the question whether data, thus collected from many villages can be pooled together for the purpose of any meaningful comparison and for drawing any general conclusion. At the same time, without systematic comparison it would not be possible to develop a general theory of any kind. However, in the present context, the major emphasis was laid on the comparison of the communication process rather than on structure, which we considered could be compared.

Participant observation : One of the most important research techniques followed by anthropologists is participant observation. "This approach involves participating in the day-to-day life of the people being studied by living with them over an extended period of time" (Olien 1978 : 19). The use of such a research method was found necessary as it is very difficult to elicit correct responses through questionnaires. At the same time our study was an exploratory one in many ways.

These five themes are similar to those indicated by Olien in his recent book *The Human Myth* (1978). In SITE social research and evaluation, we had used these five specialities of anthropology in various ways as discussed later in the book.

In the past, majority of the TV summative evaluations consisted of quantitative 'impact' or 'effect' studies conducted with the help of sample surveys. Earlier surveys conducted in rural India had serious methodological problems in eliciting correct responses (Rudolph and Rudolph 1960 : 745-55 and Elder 1968: 173-186). Therefore, it was felt that a method that allows deep probing and understanding of the communication process *insitu* should be followed as an alternative approach for social evaluation of SITE. We thought that 'impact' survey would only allow a probe into some pre-determined specific areas, rather than the exploration of the wide canvas of human behaviour. In other words, instead of measuring the impact of TV in some specific areas, an attempt should be made to understand the role and process of TV communication while focusing on man in his totality. In order to analyse communication process as a whole, it became imperative to follow a 'research design' which would allow diachronic observations. It is a safe assumption that TV messages are interpreted and understood within the cultural context. Therefore, it is essential to discover these cultural judgements and various categories of TV messages for contextual interpretation. Having this consideration in view, a methodological strategy, yielding the necessary data, became a challenge for us.

Emic approach allows the researcher to participate, observe and study the cultural categories in which a 'linguistic group' categorizes, classifies and interprets a new message (Harris 1968 : 416-418). It is for this reason, that an attempt was made to collect data as best as possible in *emic* categories. So, at the empirical level, all daily observations, notes and diaries were written in the mother-tongue of the anthropologists and in the languages of the village under study. The nine villages, which have been studied belong to seven states. Therefore, it is logical to raise the question whether data, thus collected, can be pooled together for the purpose of any meaningful comparison, and for drawing any general conclusions. A number of questions can be raised against any comparison, which also happens to be a controversial issue in anthropology. However, in the present context, the major emphasis was laid on the comparison of the process rather than on the structure. However, in order to provide a meaningful contextual understanding, it would be essential to have a brief description of Satellite Instructional Television Experiment's or SITE's aim and scope and configuration.

Satellite Instructional Television Experiment (SITE) : aims and objectives

SITE is one of the biggest technologically most advanced techno-social experiments in the direct broadcasting for education and development. It is also one of the largest Indo-US experiments in communication conducted so far. "In this project, the experimenters' main objective was to provide instantaneous information for national development to those who otherwise would have been deprived to such information for many years to come due to technological constraints" (Agrawal 1978 :1).

The specific social goals of SITE were to improve the general primary education, provide teacher training, help to improve agricultural practices, health, hygiene and nutrition and contribute to family planning of villages as well as provide a national integration. It was expected that television messages telecast through satellite and received on direct broadcasting system in the villages would help achieve these goals.

SITE was conducted for one year from 1, August 1975 to 31, July 1976. It was conducted in 2330 villages spanning 20 districts of six economically backward states of India referred to as clusters. These states were Andhra Pradesh, Bihar, Karnataka, Madhya Pradesh, Orissa and Rajasthan. In each village, a Direct Reception System (DRS) television was installed in a public place for community viewing. This special television had basically three elements—a three metre chicken mesh parabolic antenna, a low noise pre-amplifier, and a conventional 61cm TV receiver. All TV sets, except 134 battery operated TV sets installed in Orissa, operated on 220 volts AC supply. In addition, approximately 504 conventional 61 cm TV sets in 335 villages were installed in Kheda district of Gujarat state which received the satellite TV signal through a rediffusion system.

Signals were beamed from Ahmedabad and Delhi earth stations to NASA's Applications Technology Satellite-6 (ATS-6) having a capacity of two audio and one video transmission. These signals were received back in the villages on direct reception system.

TV programmes were produced by Doordarshan's (Indian government run television authority) three base production units located in Delhi, Cuttack and Hyderabad. The science education programmes for school children and Gujarati programmes for Kheda were produced by the Space Applications Centre's Ahmedabad and Bombay studios. The programmes were telecast in the morning and in the evening in all the clusters, excluding Kheda where it was telecast only in the evening.* In the morning a one-and-half hour programme in Hindi, Kannada, Oriya and Telugu languages for 22½ minutes each were telecast for school children in the age group of 5-12 years. In the evening, a two-hour programme in the same four languages (20 minutes for each cluster) for adult viewers were telecast. A half-hour national programme (partly live) were telecast in Hindi for all clusters from Delhi earth station whereas all other programmes were telecast from Ahmedabad earth station.

During the SITE year, telecast reliability was above 99 per cent. More than 80 per cent direct reception systems were functioning at any given time in the villages.

There were two most important dimensions that are crucial for the understanding of Anthropologists' role in satellite communication research and evaluation. These were : (1) the satellite had the capacity to transmit messages simultaneously to all the six clusters of India, and (2) it had the capacity to provide one picture (video) and two languages (audio).

*It included half-hour National Hindi and half-hour Gujarati programmes.

Anthropologists viewed communication as a process in the broad cultural context and objectives of the holistic study were defined.

General objectives

- To study the process of existing rural communication.
- To study the role of TV as a new medium of communication in SITE instructional areas.
- To study the process of change brought about by TV in the rural structure at micro-level.

Specific objectives

Based on the general objectives some of the specific objectives of the study were :

- To study the process of cultural communication.
- To study the various existing channels of rural and developmental communication.
- To study the utilization pattern of existing channels of communication for developmental and non-developmental activities in SITE villages.
- To study the rediffusion process of developmental messages at pre-SITE, during-SITE and post-SITE.
- To study the substitution process, if any, of existing channels of communication by TV introduction.
- To study the positive and negative roles played by TV in accelerating rural development in areas of agriculture, family planning, health, hygiene and nutrition.
- To study micro-level changes brought about by TV in the village culture.
- To study the aspects of TV programme components.
- To study the impact of one picture-two-language TV programming in Andhra Pradesh/Karnataka villages.
- To evaluate the impact of the national programmes in Hindi and non-Hindi speaking villages.
- To study the process of adoption of developmental messages.
- To study the existing pattern of primary education in SITE villages and impact of TV on the school going children between 5-12 years age group.
- To study the pattern of communication in the above areas with special reference to females.

A major criticism of the holistic study is that it has very little generalizing value and thus, is of no use to planners or decision-makers. Looking into SITE research, one may like to pose one question—whether the study of nine villages having a total population of 12000-15000 provides a better sample or a couple of thousand respondents selected from some 100 villages? Careful analysis indicates that these two types of samples provided complementary rather than contradictory inputs for planning and decision making; and in their own right are equally valid methods of research. In communication research, "illuminative evaluation" essentially a holistic approach has started gaining more acceptance among professionals.

In this chapter an attempt was made to describe the historical development of anthropological study in communication research with special reference to SITE. The next two chapters will present the methodology of the field work.

CHAPTER TWO

METHODOLOGICAL STRATEGY FOR COMMUNICATION RESEARCH

by

BINOD C. AGRAWAL

The Holistic Study Team

METHODOLOGICAL STRATEGY FOR COMMUNICATION RESEARCH

—BINOD C. AGRAWAL

IN THE previous chapter an attempt was made to discuss the theoretical and the methodological issues involved in conducting holistic study. Within this theoretical and methodological framework, there were four steps involved in conducting the evaluative study, which will be presented in detail in this chapter. These four steps include (a) Selection of a village in each cluster, (b) Methods and techniques to be followed in data collection, (c) Nature and quality of data to be collected, (d) Specific areas, in which the focus should be directed towards obtaining answers to the specific questions of the evaluative study.

VILLAGE SELECTION

Anthropological and sociological literature indicates that the 'real village', and the 'revenue village' represent two levels of sociological reality. For TV installation, the revenue village was considered as a spatial unit, as most of the official records, like census and revenue, are only available for the revenue village. It had become amply clear to the village selection team that a large revenue village, say in Bihar or Rajasthan, generally consists of a number of satellite villages, in addition to the 'main village'. The entire revenue village was named after the main village in the census. Such a problem is not uncommon for the student of social sciences conducting research in village India. In order to bridge the gap between what seemed to be a meaningful spatial entity like a village, as defined in the anthropological and sociological literature, and the revenue village, a pragmatic decision was taken. Based on the assumption that those who lived near the TV centre in the spatially defined boundary would come to view TV. Such a spatial boundary should be studied. The other settlements falling within the same revenue village are referred to as (in official records) *Dhani* in Rajasthan, *Tola* or *Parwa* in Bihar, *Kamp* in Karnataka. *Dera* in Madhya Pradesh, and *Sivaru* or *Madira* in Andhra Pradesh. These settlements referred to as 'fringe' settlements were not the main focus of the study, though the persons who came frequently from these settlements to watch TV had transactions with the main settlement.

From the universe of 2330 SITE villages (scattered in six clusters), and 335 villages of Kheda, the most important question was as to how to select a representative village in each cluster for this study. The problem of village selection became more complex with the knowledge that most of the SITE villages could not meet the basic characteristics of a 'little community', viz., *small and homogenous population*, all pervading self sufficiency and spending life from cradle to grave in one place. However, conceptually, a TV village can be considered as a 'whole system' in which various parts are inter-related and inter-connected. (Foster 1969; Redfield 1955).

Two stage sampling procedure was followed in the selection of villages from each cluster including Kheda. In the first stage, the districts were selected, and in the second stage, the villages were selected. (This criteria narrowed down the choice of selection of the villages. Still, it was fairly difficult to choose one village in each cluster based on the above criteria). First, it was decided to select a district in each cluster. Thus, seven districts had to be selected from within the list of 21 districts, that is, atleast one from each cluster. In the case of Gujarat, the question of selection of a district did not arise because Kheda was the only district under the experiment.

In the case of the other six clusters, in order to provide fair representation, it was argued that in three *clusters*, the villages should be selected from the districts *having the largest number of* SITE villages, and in the other three clusters, the village had to be selected from the districts having the *smallest number* of SITE villages. Accordingly, in the states of Andhra Pradesh, Bihar and Orissa, the districts of Hyderabad, Muzaffarpur and Sambalpur respectively, were selected in the first category. Whereas in Karnataka, Madhya Pradesh and Rajasthan districts of Raichur, Bilaspur and Sawai Madhopur respectively, were selected in the second category. Thus, it was possible to narrow the range of choice.

Criteria

For village selection five criteria were used. These were :

(1) The population size of the village should range between 1000-1500, so that it could be efficiently observed by a single anthropologist.

(2) The village should be multi-jati (consisting of more than one Hindu jati).

(3) The village should be within a distance of 20 to 30 km. from an urban centre, preferably, the cluster headquarters or the maintenance sub-centre.

(4) The villages should be, as far as possible, least affected by urban influence.

(5) One of these villages should be predominantly tribal, and if possible with a battery operated television set.

Having selected the districts, all villages with a population of 1000-1500 were separated and then plotted on the map to see if they met the distance criteria. An exception on the distance criteria was made in the case of Sambalpur, Orissa cluster where 134 battery operated sets were deployed within a distance of 15 kilometres from the maintenance sub-centres. Therefore, the distance criteria was relaxed in the case of Sambalpur. With the help of *Census Hand Books*, 1971 (refer Census 1971) efforts were also made to find out the percentage of Scheduled Caste and Scheduled Tribe population in the villages to fulfil the second and fifth criteria.

After this initial tentative selection, the anthropologists went to the field with a list of nine to ten problem villages, from which a village was to be selected after the first visit. An information sheet was prepared and was given to the anthropologists for data collection. This was essentially meant for actual verification of the data already available in Census 1971, and collected by the village selection team. The visit was also meant to check whether accommodation would be available and whether the villagers would be willing to accept an anthropologist for a year and a half.

After the actual field visits, which took about a week, the anthropologists returned to Ahmedabad. Based on the data, discussions were held and a village was selected in each cluster. The selection was done by the process of elimination. An exception to this rule was Ismailpur village in Bihar, where the first visit indicated that none of the nine villa ges visited were suitable for study. The whole process was repeated for Bihar and two new villages were selected, between which a final selection was to be made after preliminary visits. These two villages fell slightly short of the population criteria, but it was assumed that the population must have increased since 1971 when the census was taken. Due to limited time at our disposal and in consultation with the village selection team, it was decided to select Ismailpur having a population of 966 according to Census 1971. Similarly two villages for the fellows of A.N. Sinha Institute of Social Studies, Patna were selected in Bihar and Rajasthan clusters.

Once the villages were selected, anthropologists were discouraged from making any changes. Even then in Madhya Pradesh, a new village Sakarra, in the same district, fulfilling the selection criteria was selected, as the two anthropologists could not do field work in the selected village of Bundela (district : Bilaspur, Madhya Pradesh). In the first village it was feared that TV would not be installed, as the transformer was stolen and the electric cables cut.

Later analysis indicated that all the nine villages selected for the study did not have 'fringe settlements' as concluded earlier. In the case of Andhra Pradesh, Bihar, Gujarat and Madhya Pradesh, the revenue village boundaries coincided with the TV village, whereas in the case of Orissa and Bihar the TV village consisted of more than one revenue village. In Orissa, part of the neighbouring revenue village Jhankarpali belongs to the Ghenupali TV village; and in Barahser and Ismailpur, Bihar, parts of other villages form the TV village boundaries. In the case of Rajasthan the villages Khedli and Bhutera have hamlets which have been considered as fringe villages, whereas, the main settlement of the villages have been considered as the TV village.

It may be mentioned, that almost all the nine selected villages fulfilled the selection criteria suggested earlier, except the criteria of distance in the case of Ismailpur, Bihar, (without a first visit the distance indicated from Muzaffarpur in the map was accepted, which is actually 37 km. Similarly, the census of Khedli and Bhutera villages, Rajasthan were 1357 and 1353 respectively according to the Census of India, 1971. But the census of the TV villages when enumerated, showed lower figures. The same holds true in the case of Ghenupali (Orissa), where the village population was indicated as 1189, according to the Census of India, 1971. In this case, part of Ghenupali and part of Jhankarpali revenue village constituted the TV village, having a population of 684 and, thus, these two villages have a lower population than initially planned for the study. It may be further mentioned that Ghenupali is a tribal village.

Training

Before discussing the actual method of data collection, it would be important to mention that attempts were made to collect uniform and comparable data from each of the villages under study. For this purpose, it was essential to give a uniform training to each of the anthropologists. Therefore, pre-data collection training was organized. The training essentially, aimed at reorienting the anthropologists to understand communication process in village India, the theoretical and methodological basis of the study and the understanding of the role of TV in a community viewing situation.

During the training, each concept that was supposed to be used in data collection was discussed and was operationally defined. This was essential as anthropologists were trained in various universities and there seemed to be no agreement on many of the concepts like jati, joint and nuclear family. Areas and priorities were defined for the purpose of data collection in the various phases of study. Before sending the team to the field, they were sent to Delhi for a week's training in National Council of Educational Research and Training (NCERT), New Delhi to learn about child psychology and how to observe child behaviour in the school. Only four out of the original nine, who completed the field work, were able to take advantage of the training as the others left the job before its completion.

After the training at Delhi, the anthropologists went to the villages to set up their residence and to start field work.

The data collection during field work was divided into three phases—(1) pre-SITE (2) SITE (3) post-SITE.

It was hoped that the process evaluative study (feedback data collection) would be done during the SITE year, whereas pre-SITE observations would provide a base-line data for the purpose of evaluation from post-SITE data. Within a single village, those who viewed TV were to be compared with those who did not view TV, for evaluation and comparison of change among viewers, before and after TV viewing.

Field work

In the first week of March, field work started as per schedule in Kawadpalley (Andhra Pradesh), Ismailpur and Barahser (Bihar), Pothnal (Karnataka), Bundela (Madhya Pradesh) and Ghenupali (Orissa), and Bhutera (Rajasthan). However, due to the non-availability of anthropologists, the field work in Dadusar and Khedli, was delayed until 1 July, 1975, and 22 October 1975 respectively.

In Khedli, the television and field work started more or less, at the same time, as TV was non-functional until 2 October 1975. In Dadusar, field work started a month prior to the date of commencement of SITE.

Teething troubles started within a few weeks of field work. The anthropologist in Karnataka felt incapacitated and it became inevitable to replace him, by 15 July 1975. In Orissa, within 10 days, it was found that the anthropologist felt that he could not live in the village due to lack of appropriate amenities and transport facilities and so he was replaced in 2 weeks by another anthropologist. In Madhya Pradesh, the anthropologist suffered from serious stomach ailments and was forced to resign. He was replaced by another anthropologist, who after shifting to Sakarra village absconded from the field and could not be traced until November 1975. Hence, no data could be collected in Sakarra village until 22 February 1976, because no one could be appointed till that day.

In Orissa village, the second anthropologist left the job after about 8 months of field work in early January, 1976. He was replaced by another anthropologist who was doing field work in another SITE evaluating project. The anthropologists, working in Madhya Pradesh and Orissa, were given two weeks training before they were sent to the field. In this way, nineteen months of continuous field work in Ismailpur, Barahser, Bhutera and Kawadpalley was done, whereas, in Pothnal and Dadusar, field work was done for 15 months. In Khedli, field work was done for a period of 11½ months. In Sakarra, field work was done for a period of eight-and-a-half months. In Ghenupali, the field work was conducted for a period of approximately 16 months, with an interruption in the months of January and February, 1976 in which three anthropologists worked.

All field work was terminated in the first week of October, 1976, approximately about two months after completion of SITE. During the entire field work, anthropologist came to Ahmedabad, thrice for the purposes of review, discussion, and for the preliminary presentation of their data, which accounted for about five to six weeks of absence from the village.

Anthropologists in the field

The anthropologists who were able to speak the local language of the villages under study, settled in the village in a house, located near the TV centre, except in Kawadpalley and Pothnal, where the residence of these anthropologists were within the TV nuclear village. They maintained a modest living in most cases. They lived in rented rooms. They lived in electrified houses as these villages were electrified, except in Ghenupali. Two anthropologists, one in Khedli and the other in Dadusar, lived in the village with their families. In Khedli, the wife of the anthropologist collected special data on the women and their communication behaviour since she was trained in the profession as well. In Sakarra and in Kawadpalley, two female anthropologists stayed for a period of about four months, beginning from June, 1976, at the fag end of field work. They also collected separate data on the women and children of the respective villages. The female anthropologist from Kawadpalley visited Pothnal also, for a period of about two weeks, to collect comparable data (in two trips) between the two villages.

All these anthropologists introduced themselves as associated with television. However, they indicated that they had nothing to do with operation, maintenance and functioning of television. This, no doubt gave an image of an 'officer' but gradually it faded as their interaction with the villagers became more intimate as can be observed in the following chapters. Anthropologists were introduced to the villagers by an important person like village head-man, president of the village panchayat (council), or through some local government officials. In all the villages except Pothnal, anthropologists were initially given help by these leaders, as most of the government officials are entertained and assisted by leaders. In the village, leaders tried to influence the anthropologists. It seems that in every case village headmen tried to patronise the anthropologists, who could succeed in maintaining their independent identity by interacting with poor and rich, and lower and higher jatis belonging to various religious groups. In every village, the anthropologists were suspected, initially, to be men from the government intelligence department.

After a few months of field work, anthropologists became part of the village and were treated as members of the village. They participated in village fairs and festivals. When they left the village, they were given a farewell similar to that of a villager leaving home permanently. Generally speaking, anthropologists established a fairly good rapport with the villagers, though a few villagers were suspicious about their activities and could not be convinced as to why an educated person would live in the village for such a long period. The anthropologists mainly participated in TV viewing throughout the year, during the morning and evening transmissions, and focused their attention on issues related to TV and communication. This did not mean that they ignored other aspects of village culture.

Pre-SITE data: Originally, it was decided to collect base line data before SITE. It was this rationale which led the anthropologists to start working in the first week of March, 1975. In the initial stage of the field work, everyone was asked to collect houeshold census and to draw the map of the TV village. The household schedule was developed in the local language for each village separately, which included damographic data on the household-operationally defined as those persons living and eating together, who may or may not be related to each other. Household census schedule also included questions related to religion and jati affiliation, language and mass media exposure. (see Appendix I)

Door-to-door census was conducted just after the beginning of the field work, which helped anthropologists to familiarize themselves with the village and build rapport with the villagers. Simultaneously a national map of the village was drawn plotting the settlement pattern of the village. Approximately, two to four weeks were needed to complete census and mapping.

In pre-SITE period, attempts were made to establish a good rapport with the villagers—experience indicated that the village leaders (elected and appointed)—acted as the bridge between the anthropologist and the villagers in the beginning which gradually dwindled as the time passed. The anthropologists mainly concentrated their energy on collecting data on the existing channels of communication in the village. This included investigating various methods that are used for the purpose of transmitting religious messages through travelling musicians and saints, collective listening of religious and mythological hymns, incoming and out-going postal mail, and a host of interpersonal channels of communication that are used in the village for the purposes of transmitting information among the relatives, friends, jati members and gossip groups.

Before the commencement of SITE, the anthropologists attended a workshop, held at Ahmedabad in which anthropologists of various university departments also participated. In the workshop, it was decided to collect data on those items which were more susceptible to change, namely, traditional communication interaction patterns and adoption behaviour in SITE instructional areas—agriculture, health, nutrition, family planning and national integration. The changes in kinship, religion and some economic aspects, such as, income, land holdings, and occupations were not expected to change within the short spell of one year and, hence, the collection of data on these items were given second priority. For this purpose, a broad outline of the areas, in which data should be collected, were sent to anthropologists in the field. (see Appendix III)

During-SITE data : By the time SITE started in the villages, except in Khedli, anthropologists were already living in the villages. Their major data collection activity centred around morning and evening TV viewing, and observation of post telecast discussions, and participation in the day-to-day life. The main aim was to discover how TV messages reached the non-television viewers in the villages. Questions asked during the investigation were—Who watched TV ? What was the sitting pattern of the viewers in the community viewing situation and how were changes, if any, taking place in the day-to-day life of the villagers as a consequence of TV viewing directly, indirectly, or incidentally.

A daily observation sheet was designed (see Appendix) to observe the changes in viewing and sitting patterns, audience size, and its composition. As the sitting pattern was, more or less, uniform during the morning transmission because of the class room viewing, a small quantum of data in the last two months of the transmission were collected. (Also see Appendices IVV to II)

After nine months of SITE exposure, in April 1976, supplementary quantitative data were collected from a sample of the adult male and female viewers of all nine villages.

Science teachers' training : One of the highlights of SITE was the Multi-media package Training programme for Science Teachers, in which TV was also used for the training, apart from radio and written material. For a period of 15 days, first in mid-October 1975, and later in July, 1976, the training was imparted. An effort was made by the anthropologists to evaluate the training programme. The broad questions investigated were : the TV utilization pattern during the training, the general observations of the training organization at the village level, and the trainees' opinions on the utility and usefulness of the training programme. This training programme was conducted in six clusters excluding Dadusar.

All anthropologists except at Dadusar, observed and participated in one of the two training programmes.* As the training programmes were similar in nature, some villages were not selected twice for the training.

In each village, the basic data was collected through participant observation and informal discussion with the trainee teachers, among whom a few were personally known to the anthropologists. Operation, co-ordination, and management

*No training programme were organized in Gujarat state.

aspects of the training were also studied in detail.

Post-SITE data collection : In post-SITE period, the routine of the anthropologists was modified as they changed their strategy of data collection. They were mostly involved in observing if there were any changes in the village after the termination of telecasts on 31 July 1976. They wanted to assess how viewers felt about the absence of TV and how they tried to readjust their evening activity schedule. A small structured schedule was used for data collection from a randomly selected sample. The anthropologists collected data from adult viewers of both sexes, children and the TV custodian in each village. (see Appendix VII)

Data from Dadusar was not collected as the telecasts were not terminated on 31 July 1976. Just three weeks before the termination of field work, the anthropologists collected the post SITE survey data from the panel of the same respondents who were interviewed during-SITE.

Special data on women : The specific data on women were collected in Khedli.* Kawadpalley, Pothnal and Sakarra by female anthropologists. The data collected by female anthropologists focused on child rearing practices, role of women in communication process at various levels in the village and observations on change as a results of TV viewing among females. They also assisted in collecting survey data from females.

Operational definitions

Prior to the field work, and during the field work, the most difficult part was, and continues to be, the definition of the various *emic* categories used for the purpose of description and analysis. The conceptual difficulty becomes more acute when the data from the seven villages have to be compared. To have conceptual clarity, operational definitions of each of the concepts have been presented and are followed throughout the report.

Village : One of the most puzzling questions is the definition of the village. As indicated earlier there are a number of definitions of the village. The term 'village' has been used

*Small quantity of data were also collected in the villages of Kawadpalley Pothnal and Sakarra by women anthropologists. But it is not discussed.

interchangeably with TV settlement and 'TV village'. Therefore, throughout this book the term village refers to 'TV-village', unless defined otherwise.

Jati : The term *jati* is used to denote an endogamous, intermarrying, extended and regional group. A similar concept also exists among non-Hindus. Therefore, term 'jati-like' will be referred to the similar non-Hindu groups.

Household : In emic term the 'family' is referred to as 'Ghar' in Hindi and Gujarati. *Gharoro* in Oriya speaking areas, *Illu* in Telugu, and *Mannethana* in Kannada. In this book the term 'household' has been used to denote *Ghar*, operationally defined as those persons living and eating together who may or may not be relatives.

Process of communication: In this study, the emphasis was on the understanding of the process of communication. According to Wallace (1970 : 100) ;

> processes have in common the property that time, and often physical space too, is a dimension of the structure, and that the structure is divided into a sequence of steps or stages corresponding to the successive values on the time/space dimension. Each stage then can be considered as a single value on a dimension that corresponds precisely in number of values to the time/space dimension ; but each of these values on the stage dimension can be decomposed into a complex structure whose matrix may be (but is not necessarily) unique to that stage.

In the communication context, the programmes shown on TV were seen by a limited number of viewers, who in turn went to the village and discussed what they had seen on TV with other non-viewers. The non-viewers, in turn, discussed with other non viewers. In this case, three-step flow of communication is indicated, with each stage defined by persons who act as mediators between the information and the receivers of the information. Certain amount of information gets modified, changed or distorted before reaching the next person. It seems that these processual structures contain three kinds of dimensions—time/space, a 'core matrix'—information that is shared by all stages, though, it may get transformed while moving from one stage to another stage, and finally the 'peripheral matrix'—television viewer/non-viewer. "The peripheral matrices are relevant only in some of the stages".

Wallace (1970 : 101) feels that "some simple structure can have only the first two stages". In the present discussion, all the three dimensions will be considered and analysed while discussing the process of communication. In most cases, it will be implicit, but from time to time, it will be made explicit.

School children : The term 'school children' refers to those who are between 5-12 years of age and who attend primary school, generally upto the 5th grade.

Adult : The term 'adult', male and female, is operationally defined as all those who are of age 15 years and above at the time of census taking of the village.

Children : From time to time, data are categorised into two major age groups—children and adults. When the term children alone is used, it refers to all those who are 14 years of age and below.

Viewers : The trem 'viewers' or 'frequent viewers' has been operationally defined as those who view TV more than four times a month.

Core viewer : The term 'core viewer' is used for those adults who viewed programmes more than two thirds of time when the TV was operational in a month.

Unit of Analysis : The analysis was done at two levels—household and village. While discussing a village most of the analyses focus around households whereas when villages were compared, the unit of comparison was the village.

CHAPTER THREE

IN THE FIELD . . .

by

BINOD C. AGRAWAL, J.K. DOSHI, K.K. VERMA AND
SASHIKALA VISWANATH

J.K. Doshi Ph.D. (Anthropology) worked as co-project leader of this study. He was born in a Rajasthan town and was educated both in Hindi and English languages.

K.K. Verma Ph.D. (Anthropology) worked as co-project leader of this study. He was born in a Bihar town and was educated both in Hindi and English languages.

Sashikala Viswanath M.A. in English literature assisted in the compilation and editing of this book. She was born in a Tamil speaking family of Madras.

An Indian Village

A typical TV viewing

IN THE FIELD . . .

—BINOD C. AGRAWAL, J.K. DOSHI,
K.K. VERMA AND SASHIKALA VISWANATH

SITE ANTHROPOLOGISTS AT WORK

IN ORDER to maintain uniformity, consistency and comparability in the data it was felt essential to provide a set of instructions to all the anthropologists. It became imperative to do so, keeping in view the varying quality of training these anthropologists have had during their post graduation. The first instruction was about the approach to field work. "Most of the books on field methods are written from the 'foreign' point of view for the study of the 'native'. Our effort will be to develop a new methodology for the study of our own people. As a member of the larger linguistic region you share most of the broad values and beliefs of your people. The most important of all is that you speak the same language as your informants speak. In other words you do not have to spend any time in learning the language. But you will have to adopt the local dictum and style of speech. Your individual social background in most cases will determine your status in the village". The assumption in this approach was that the anthropologist, as an individual, would in the course of time build relationships with the villagers and would be viewed in a perspective that would yield deeper understanding of the village life of which they were a part in most cases.

Being a native anthropologist he/she may be questioned about 'objectivity' and accused of the influence of personal bias in her/his field work. The anthropologists were asked to argue on the grounds of the effect of good training and knowledge of the local language which would minimize the bias. Afterall,

* The original instruction is provided in Appendix-II.

anthropological field work is an individualized personal experience.

The anthropologists were asked to avoid taking sides in village feuds and to maintain a neutral position, if asked to intervene by the villagers. Their 'job of observation' would have to be situated in the centre of the village. Anthropologists were asked to spend a small amount for living expenditure equivalent to that afforded by a University Junior Research Fellow and to avoid expectations of any special treatment from the villagers.

Guide for writing of field notes and diaries

The field diary of an anthropologist is the basic document which contain all the data collected by him/her, and hence careful confidential preservation of the diary was essential. The anthropologists were asked to give precise and detailed descriptions of their observations the essence of anthropological field work. Facts and interpretations were to be written separately and conversations to be noted in the vernacular language. Two kinds of field notes were to be observed, (a) taking notes on the spot and, (b) writing a detailed daily diary. The notes may be written in situations such as festivals and ceremonies and while observing or talking to the villagers. A major portion of the field data may be collected in this way. On occasions such as a funeral ceremony, it may be extremely difficult to take notes on the spot and hence one can make field notes in pocket diaries in such situations.

Daily field diary

Anthropologists were instructed to write their field diary everyday in which (a) detailed notes of observations, (b) field notes on discussions and conversations, (c) details of interpersonal communication, gossips, fold history and similar events and (d) specific details of special events like marriage, and festivals were to be noted. Special reference about the main field of study for instance, the details about the process of message diffusion, various kinds of channels of communication were to be described in detail. It was also pointed to them that it was important to distinguish between *observation* and *interpretation*. Theory and fact should not be merged. A 'theoretical model' should be constructed and be put to test.

This should be written separately and only after recording the facts.

Language

"In the process of translation from one language to another, one lose's the meaning and expression. Secondly, the linguistic ability of the individual anthropologist also influences the translation. It is recommended that you should try to write your field notes in the local language as far as possible. You must write all specific terms in the local language, like kinship terms. It will help you in getting good quality data. Later at the time of report writing we will together translate the field diary into English." These instructions were given to anthropologists.

Setting up

The first question that the anthropologist may encounter would be 'who are you' and 'what is the purpose of your stay in the village?'. Your answer will be that 'you want to study the impact of TV on village life and that you belong to Research and Evaluation Cell of Space Applications Centre, Ahmedabad'. In case of Research Fellows of A.N. Sinha Institute, they will associate themselves with A.N. Sinha Institute, Patna. Please repeat the same statement no matter how many times you are asked this question. Do not feel irritated to repeat. For heavens sake *do not change* your statement. You will be asked about your salary. Tell the truth about your basic salary.

The anthropologists were asked not to take many obligations, and if so to reciprocate. Their homes were to be set up independently which would help them in their field work as well to maintain an independent position in the village.

Camera and its use

The anthropologists were given a camera and asked to use 120 and 35 mm films which would be given to them. The camera was to be used for taking photographs of rituals, festivals, marriages, death and such other events. However, the anthropologists were asked to be cautious about the villagers' sentiments in the use of camera. For instance, taking photographs of the temple deities and many ceremonies may not be allowed.

They were asked to refuse the villagers if they requested for snap shots of themselves. And if the anthropologist were to concede he/she was to pay for the film. They were also asked to refuse payment from the villagers for the photographs.

Specific instructions about processing of the films were also given—"Please mark every film role. Send it to cluster headquarters where you should get it processed. Keep your negatives in negative files properly induced. Write details of the negative content. It will help you while writing the report. In case you take some colour transparencies, get them processed through associate scientist. Please take as many photographs as possible. Be clear in your mind why you want to take a particular photograph. This will help you later in writing and also using these photographs instead of one. 'Action pictures' would be the best."

The taperecorder

The taperecorder, a tool for data collection could be used for interviews and for recording a song or a dialogue. It could also be used for recording reobtain data and hence function as a tool for ensuring accurate data. However, the anthropologists were also informed about its limitations as well as given instructions as to the methods for its use.

"Informants become conscious of a taperecorder which may alter the flow of conversation. They may feel very suspicious and refuse to speak. On other occasions they may want you to replay the conversations. In each case, the use of taperecorder may be a hindrance in your field work.

"Keeping a proper index of the tapes would be another problem."

"Many times after the recording is done you may forget to write other details which may effect later analysis."

The following instructions were given about the use of the taperecorder :

— To use the taperecorder only after developing a good rapport in the village.
— To give data about place of interview, subject/topic of discussion, and tape number. This exercise was to be repeated at the end of the interview.

— Space on the top of the cassette should be used for identification.
— A separate operation manual on the use of taperecorder provided to the anthropologists, was to be read carefully.

Pre-SITE field work

The first few weeks of residence in the village would involve a plan of work, which would allow the anthropologist to observe the physical and social arrangement of the village. This was to be done by mapping the village, making a household census, using census schedule (see Appendix-I). Geneologies would provide the necessary information regarding the relationships among the various households which would be useful in tracing out the social contexts of the villagers.

A map showing the physical features—streams, springs, streets, hills, rivers, temples, ponds and fields was to be drawn, which would help in identifying the property, neighbourhood, direction of village growth as well as in taking census. The anthropologists were asked to note down the available information regarding the various diseases, the ceremonies and celebrations connected with them and the deities associated with the ceremonies. This information was to be annexed with the information collected from the health centres, if any, falling within the vicinity of the village.

SITE

By the time anthropologists would be able to locate the key informants and leaders in the village before the commencement of TV programmes. Relationships with key informants should ensure a discrete silence about every interview and observational data. It would also be unwise and unethical to try to trade off the information from one informant to another, in the hope of gaining something more.

They were asked to play the role of a participant observer, and to note down the reactions of the TV viewers. SITE would envisage of two sets of programmes, morning programmes for the school going children in the age groups of five to eleven and the evening programme for adults, relating to rural development programme. The anthropologists were advised to conduct the interviews in the morning in order to discuss the overnight programmes. The interview timings would have to be at the convenience of the villagers. While conducting interviews with the children they could 'act' the role of a child and discuss the programme in such a manner, that would provide them with sufficient data. These interviews could be done before 12'O clock. The anthropologists were advised to spend the day in the field, where the villagers may be working.

The information diffusion to neighbouring villages could be recorded by visiting the neighbouring villages at their convenient time. Record of the visitors from the neighbouring villages for TV viewing should be maintained. They would be contacted in their villages which will allow for understanding intervillage channels of communications.

Post-SITE

By the end of SITE the anthropologists would be aware of the various communication channels, the adaption and diffusion processes and impact of TV programmes in the various spheres of village life.

Post-SITE village study would aim at finding out the impact of TV programmes and how long it would last in the village. The anthropologists may find time during the phase between SITE and post-SITE, which would be two to three months. During this period, the anthropologist may be writing his reports, after which he would return to the field. They were asked to observe the impact of SITE, during this period with respect to the information and its impact on their daily life, diffusion of information and the effect of SITE on their culture.

Termination of field work

Though it is common knowledge that the anthropologist's stay in the village is temporary, an atmosphere would prevail, wherein the villagers belief would be that the anthropologists would reside here permanently. At the time of departure, they may face constraints and hence they were advised to leave calmly.

CHAPTER FOUR

THE OLD NIZAM VILLAGE

by

M.V.T. RAJU

M.V.T. Raju, after the completion of this project got his Ph.D. from Andhra University and began teaching in Satya Sai Baba College, Anantapur Andhra Pradesh. At present, he is a lecturer in the College, in the Department of Sociology. Raju was born and brought up in a telugu speaking family of Andhra Pradesh. He was educated in this state, Telugu English being the medium of instruction in school and college.

Anthropologist's at work

Female anthropologist participating in agricultural activities

THE OLD NIZAM VILLAGE

—M.V.T. RAJU

ABOUT THE VILLAGE

KAWADPALLEY is situated on the Deccan Plateau in Hyderabad district, Andhra Pradesh. It can be reached by travelling 20 km east of Hyderabad on the National Highway No. 9 and proceed from here through on all weather kutcha road for 3 kms in the northern direction. Kawadpalley is surrounded by a number of villages situated within two or three kilometres. The village can be cited from a distance by the imposing temple which stands on the opposite side of the kutcha road. This village has a population of 1089 distributed in 221 households. Hindus form the majority of the population while the Muslims are a minority. Almost three fourths of the village population live in houses built with mud walls.

Entering the village

My first visit to Kawadpalley was on March 3, 1975. I reached Abdullapur Mett from Hyderabad, a junction from where a kutcha road deviated towards Kawadpalley from the National Highway No.9. Having arrived here, I got off the bus and stood gazing around me for a few minutes, wondering how to proceed from here; when I met a boy, thirteen years of age, returning to his home in Kawadpalley from Bataringaram in bullock cart. He offered me a ride which I accepted gladly. Reaching the village, I enquired about Anant Reddy, the person whom I had been asked to contact by my supervisors. I was given directions to his home. Reaching his home, I bid *Namaskaram*, folding my palms together, addressing myself to the elderly lady who received me and said, "I am looking for a person called Anant Reddy. Can I see him?"

The lady whom I assumed rightly to be his mother informed

me that he was in the field and that she would inform him about my visit. Meanwhile, a person from the Gudali jati introduced himself and offered assistance in finding accommodation.

Anant Reddy arrived greeting me with a *Namaskaram* with palms folded together. He stated—"It is very difficult to find accommodation for you and there is only one house in the village where you can reside. I can take you there". We began walking towards the house. The owner of the house was a woman of Gudali jati. The house had a long room with no windows and facilities for outlet for water. The absence of windows made the room appear dark. But on learning that this was the only house available, I accepted it and settled the rent. After

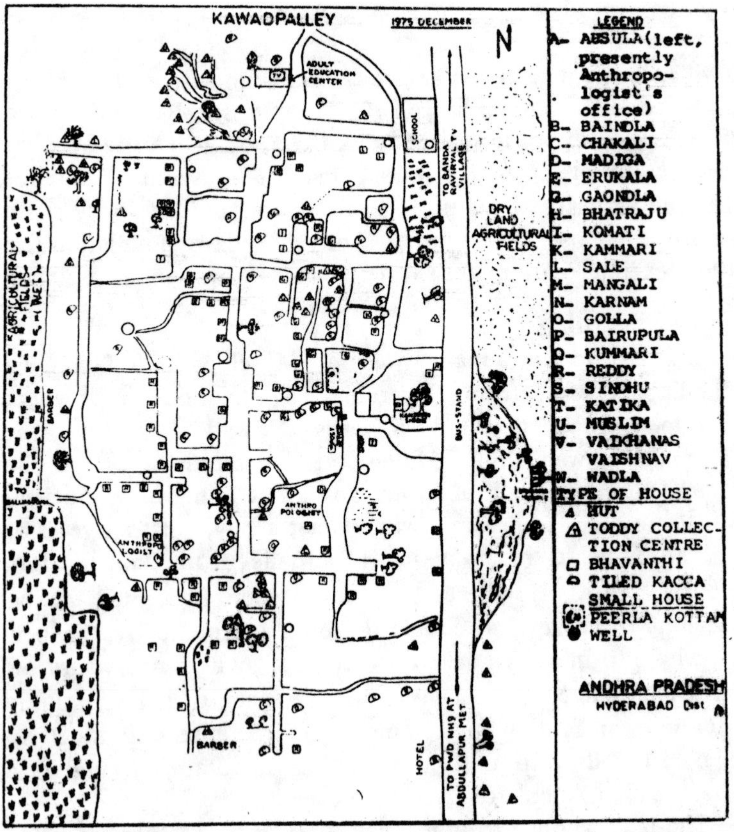

Village map of Kawadpalley

my first visit on March 3, 1975 I made two more visits. During the two visits I met the *Sarpanch* (village chief) and the Police Patel (police in charge of the village). I spoke to them about the purpose of my visit—"I am from SITE, and I am here to conduct a research study". They promised their co-operation and help and bade me their best wishes.

On March 8, 1975, I reached Kawadpalley from Hyderabad and shifted to my new residence. The associate scientists drove down to Kawadpalley in a jeep which caused a stir for it was uncommon to find motor vehicles in the village. We walked through the village streets introducing ourselves to whomever we met. I had on my earlier visits spoken little or nothing to the villagers except greeting them with a *Namaskaram*.

Introduction with villagers

In the first two weeks of my stay in Kawadpalley, my initial attempt was to prepare a rough schedule for my field work and to intermingle with the villagers. In doing so, I learnt about the existing social situation, the subtle factional politics and about the leaders of the village who were reluctant to meet me.

In the evenings, I often had a gathering in my house. The youngsters belonging to the Gudali jati would spend their evenings with me, talking for long hours. In drawing a comparison between the Gaondla jati and Gudali jati, I observed that the literacy rate and the economic status of the Gudali jati was high. I had met many members of the Gudali jati, since they had been my initial acquaintance. The other numerically dominant jati in the village was the Gaondla. I tried to identify the important members of the Gaondla jati. But this seemed difficult to do so. It was only after my first week of stay, that I learnt about their occupation—that of toddy tapping and this task demanded their absence from their homes till late evenings. Learning about their afternoon siesta, I decided to meet them in their field. I also met members of other jatis. The response of the Madiga jati (Scheduled Caste) was very encouraging for I secured their trust and confidence.

Trying to build a rapport with the villagers was not easy. Initially, some of the villagers suspected me to be a spy or CID; (a person from Central Intelligence Department). Their suspicion was affirmed when Dr. Binod C. Agrawal, the project leader visited after a few weeks of my stay. He had, during this occasion, parked his jeep ahead of the village before entering, and carried a camera with him while walking through the streets of the village. Similarly two young Madiga youth thought that I was a government official, campaigning for family planning.

On the other hand, the members of the upper jati had complaints about my visits to the houses of the Madiga jati. They asked me to invite them to my residence instead of making personal visits to their homes. But my curtness in retorting to such statements subdued them and gradually led the conversation to other topics. However, my ease in intermingling with the villagers dispelled their fears and suspicions and in time, I was able to win acceptance. This then, was my threshold in the first few weeks of my stay in Kawadpalley.

My home in Kawadpalley

Within the first few weeks, I settled in my home in Kawadpalley. The landlady, a person brimming with warmth and cheer helped me in the housework and made delicious *rotis* for dinner. I purchased milk from the village, and the other household provisions including kerosene from Hyderabad. I had also got two stoves and a pressure cooker in order to save time while cooking. My house had no electricity. Hence, my neighbours extended a line connection to my home. Since this was done without authorisation, I had to consult the Electricity Department officials.

After a few months, I shifted to a fairly decent house located in the heart of the village. This house opened to a street which was a focal point for travellers from other villages to stop midway to their destination. I could thus get a view of the hustle and bustle of village life. The house overlooked a well, where women came to draw water and hence I could observe the pattern of social transactions among the women. I continued to occupy my residence on the outskirts, using it as a kitchen and used the new one for my sleeping quarters. I did this as a matter of convenience as well as a strategy to maintain the old ties with my landlady.

In order to present an image of myself as a member of the village community, I adorned the village costume, a *lungi* and a shirt and in my visits to the school I wore trousers, for the school teacher were trousers. This distinction in dress was clearly marked in the village, highlighting the significance of the educated individual.

Living a day in Kawadpalley

The day would begin with a cup of morning tea. I would then stroll through the village streets, observing the pace of village life, the social and interpersonal transactions among the villagers, the slow and steady stealth by which the execution of morning tasks were carried out by the villagers.

This then was a typical morning in Kawadpalley. During the pre-SITE and the post-SITE phase, I would return from my stroll, have a bath and then set out to meet Gaondla men returning from their morning's toddy tapping. Mid-day was the time to participate in gossip sessions in tea shops and in the streets. Then, spending a little time to make notes and to rest, I would once again spend my late afternoons conversing with the villagers on various issues. Late nights were also spent talking to villagers who assembled in my home, a regular occurrance which had started from the beginning of my field work.

During the SITE phase, I would return early from my morning stroll to cook my meals and then go to school to view morning transmission for school children. I spent the rest of the day interviewing respondents about the TV programmes. In the evenings and late nights after TV transmssion, I would sit for long hours chatting with the villagers who would visit me in my home.

Three factors which contributed to improving my relationship with the villagers and build closer ties was the use of my camera and tape recorder as well as my role of being a supplier of medicines. The villagers, specially the children would gather around me whenever I stepped out with a camera, requesting me to take their photographs. The glee and gaity in their faces as they approached me always touched me deep within and I could never refuse them. But I could not distribute copies of the prints and thus I had to apologetically state that I couldn't do so and that they could only have a look at them and return it back. These requests were ineffective and they continued to ask for the prints. In the end I had to be firm and a little harsh, and this had the needed effect.

The taperecorder was also a useful asset in building relationships. The women would gather in my home and sing songs which I would record and replay. This happened frequently, especially on festive occasions like the Buktama festival. On replaying the tapes the women expressed their delight, for they were awe-struck about the reproduction of their voices. I also used the taperecorder for interviews.

The M/s. J. and J. Dechane, a medical firm in Hyderabad had patent remedies for common ailments like fever, cold, cough, and diarrhoea. Keeping a stock of these medicines I distributed it to the villagers whenever they were in need and hence found an opportunity to learn about the health situation of the village. In the process, I made many friends in the village.

Participation in village life

I played the role of participant-observer in the village affairs. I avoided involvement in the village feuds and issues of panchayat conflicts. But on one occasion, towards the end of my field work, I intervened in the village feud between two villagers and stopped one of them in reporting to the police, thus avoiding the involvement of the whole village in a dispute. On occasions such as marriages and festivals, my role as a photographer or as an assistant in serving food and doing odd jobs made my participation a welcome presence.

Image of the anthropologist in the villagers' mind

During my field work, I went out of the village on several occasions. Important among these were my visits to Lucknow and Ahmedabad. After return, I was asked.

> "Where have you been for so long?" to which I would reply, "Ahmedabad".
> "How did you travel?"
> "I travelled in a train."
> "But where did you cook your food when you travelled for so many days?"

I had to explain about my journey in detail and they listened with fascination. They wondered about my infrequent visits to my native home for I had during my stay of one and a half years in Kawadpalley visited my home only once. They pointed out that the youth or Kawadpalley who were working outside the village returned every month and hence it was impossible for them to comprehend my absence from my native home for so long.

My presence acted as a moral influence in the village, though I did not in any way deliberately state of verbalise my opinions. For instance, my presence compelled the school teacher to carry out her task of operating the television. Earlier, she had often neglected her responsibilities and duties. The development officer hardly visited Kawadpalley and I was told by the villagers that this was due to my increasing rapport with the villagers which they resented. Thus, my relations with the government officials were strained though the villagers treated me with respect, and had high regards for me.

Living as a bachelor in Kawadpalley, I was often allured by the rustic charm and beauty of the young maidens. Yet, I withheld my emotions and feelings to live up to the image of the reverend and the pious human being that the villagers claimed to me. Envious of my popularity in the village, two youngsters spread a rumour about my association with the women in my neighbourhood. But this bit of gossip was soon retaliated by assurances regarding my morality, by my companions and the rumour thereby subsided.

In my fieldwork, I often met with counter claims and counter questions regarding my personal life. Keeping in mind, my role as an anthropologist, I decided to speak about myself, for it satisfied the villagers, thereby building closer ties. I often narrated incidents about my village, spoke about my life style, family life, agricultural practices and the mode of labour in my village. This provided them a chance to draw a comparison and thereby inform me with details of their own village and their personal life. This new role of being a person speaking about my personal life helped me in building relationships with members of different jatis.

Informants

I found many villagers willing to help and co-operate in providing the data or information that I needed. They showed enthusiasm in helping me with any particular task in my field work. Among the women, six of them provided crucial assistance and served as good informants. Their initiative encouraged the participation of many young girls to sing folk songs on festive occasions which I recorded. The young men also helped me in various ways and provided information on many issues. I found the assistance of Anant Reddy, Shankar, Premaiah, Chinayadi Reddy, Police Patel, Mali Patil and an old man Barrak Mulliah, Irigi Pentiah, Butchi Reddy, Tulsavala and Chintakinda Sattri Reddy, crucial and significant.

Visitors

During my field work, I had a few visitors. The associate scientist visited once in two months. The project leader visited Kawadpalley twice and Dr. J.K. Doshi and Dr K.K. Verma, the co-project leaders, visited once during the course of my stay. Prof Yash Pal's and a half hour stay in Kawadpalley was an event, beckoning the whole village to my home. The technical personnel visited me often when they called on the neighbouring villages of Kawadpalley. They assisted by helping to bring kerosene tins from the city.

The last days in Kawadpalley

The villagers learnt that I would soon be leaving Kawadpalley when the television would be removed.* I however, assured them that I would stay for another two months, since my attachment to them was as intense as theirs. They were perturbed and sad about my leaving. They said : "Raju, why don't you cultivate a piece of land here and stay with us? We would love to have you with us".

While initially, it had taken me time to win acceptance from the villagers, I had, during mid-way of my fieldwork, become a good friend and came to be addressed by my first name, 'Raju' The last days in Kawadpalley ware painful. I experienced feelings of regret at the thought of departing, and pain and sorrow at having to bid the villagers goodbye, even more so, the villagers'

*After the termination of SITE, on 31st July 1976, the television sets were gradually withdrawn from each village as there was no transmission thereafter.

pathos and sorrow which they expressed with a blatant frankness and authenticity touched the core of my being. The letter of termination from SITE, Ahmedabad, reached me in September 1975. During this time, I was conducting the T2 Survey.

CHAPTER FIVE

A VILLAGE BY THE KOSI RIVER

by

M.N. JHA

Magnanand, Jha, M.A, Ph.D. in Anthropology from Ranchi University, worked on this project as a Fellow of A.N. Sinha Institute of Social Studies, Patna. After completion of this work, he worked in a collaborative action research project. Presently he is Audience Research Officer AIR Patna. He was born and brought up in a Maithili speaking family of Bihar. The medium of instruction in school was Hindi.

A VILLAGE BY THE KOSI RIVER

—M.N. JHA

ABOUT THE VILLAGE

BARAHSER is located in Kahará block of the district of Saharsa in Bahar State. The headquarters of the block is still at Saharsa 32 km south of the village. The village lies in the plain of Koshi and was flooded almost everv year prior to the construction of Koshi embankment in 1957. To reach Barahser one can either take a bus from Saharsa town to Supaul, the sub-divisional town, or go upto the nearest railway station at Panchgachhia, 8 kms east from Barahser. A kutcha (mud) road runs from Barahser to the railway station at Panchgachhia. These is no transport available from the railway station. Only two buses ply on Saharsa—Supaul road and there are also irregular. This settlement is divided into five *Tolas* (wards) comprising 219 households of different jatis.

Entering the village

My first visit to Barahser was on March 2, 1975. The gram sevak (village worker) of Saharsa accompanied me. During the course of the journey, the *Gram Sevak* began speaking about the Barahser. He told that the village was a disturbed area due to the rising tensions among the village factions. My first impression, on entering the village was not very pleasant. I almost made up my mind not to stay in Barahser for my field work, looking at the location of the settlement in the lowland,the dirty pond and the unhealthy environment. However, as a matter of procedure, I contacted the Mukhia (village head), introduced myself and asked him to help me in finding accommodation. He stated that I could stay in the village library and though this was in a dilapidated condition he promised to set it right.

After making these arrangements, I returned to Saharsa, determined not to conduct my field work in Barahser. I visited the other seven villages, which had been suggested as sample villages for the holistic study. The village Baidnathpour appealed to me for it had a community hall, maintained in a good condition. The village school teacher, Mukti Yadava, whom I contacted, assured me that the Mukhia would allow me to reside here. After a survey of all the villages, I returned to Patna. I met Professor Sachchidananda* to whom I gave an account of my survey. Professor Sachchidananda selected Barahser for my field work. On my protesting to his decision, he explained that TV would have an important role to play in a factional village.

I reached Barahser on March 11, 1975 with my luggage. I was scheduled to conduct my field work for eighteen months. Though my initial plans had been that I would reside in the library, it happened by chance that during the course of my field work, I stayed as a guest in the Mukhia's residence. Arriving at Barahser, the Mukhia met me near the library. He said that the library premises was not ready and hence offered me a room in his home. I agreed, for I had no choice.

I found, however, that this arrangement was indeed a good decision for I was able to observe and learn about the village factions from this location. The Mukhia's house was situated at Dakhinwari Tola. Villagers from the main settlement and adjacent settlements often visited the Mukhia. I got an insight into the local politics. I learnt that the government sponsored Gram Panchayat was functioning under the Communist Party of India leadership. I also learnt about the role of *opinion* leader and political leaders of the village. My neighbour, Jamunashankar was an opinion leader whose activities were a hinderance to the unity of the village.

My field work

My knowledge of the existing culture and the local language, Maithili was adequate to begin field work. The three weeks stay in the beginning enabled me to locate the important centres from where messages were being diffused in the village.

When I began field work as an outsider, I was rather lost.

* Prof. Sachchidananda was Project Director of this study.

I asked the Mukhias as to how I should go about it. The Mukhia advised me to make friends with persons closely associated with the *Thakur bari* (House of Thakur) *Bhairabasthan* (Seat of Bhairab) and *Baital chauraha* (Baital crossing) as well as those who visited the local market regularly. I did so, the data collected through participation in their conversation became the most important aspect of my filed work. It revealed the entire gamut of interpersonal communication in the village, for instance, the location, the ways and means and the time in which messages were being communicated among villagers.

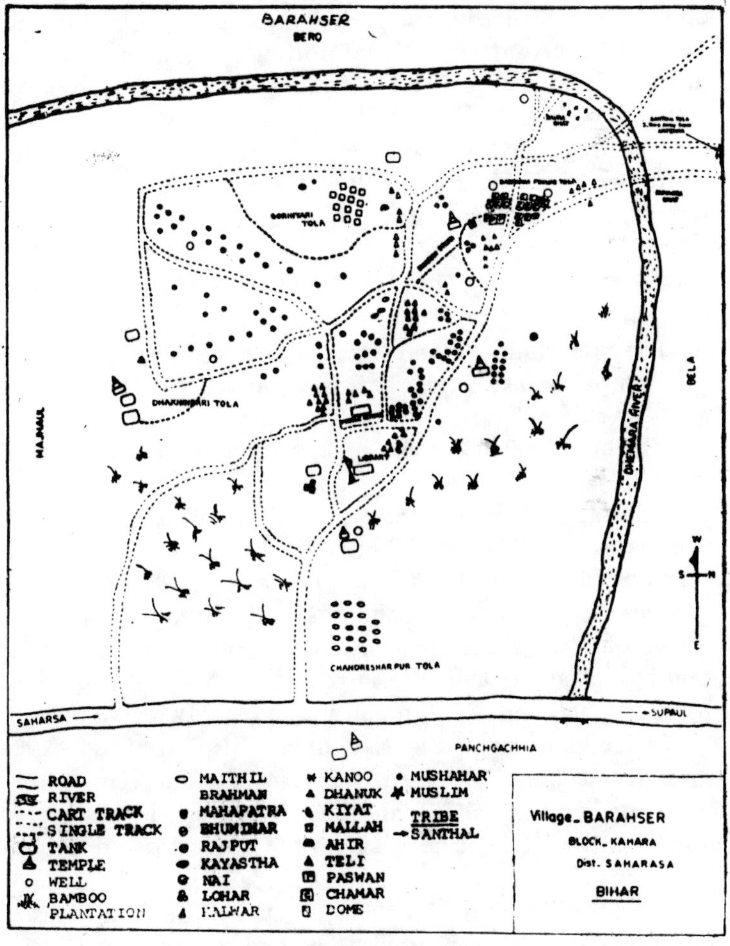

Village map of Bar ahser

I also participated in TV viewing, during SITE for understanding the audience' interest, attitudes and reactions towards a particular TV programme. I participated in their discussion of the programmes during broadcast, as well as in the villagers' homes. I would sit near the *Ghrua* (fire) along with the villagers during a village meeting which gave me an insight into the political, social and economic life of the village.

Participation in children's play, particularly *Kabbaddi* (game) proved very useful for me as I could find out their attitude towards the adoption of new rules of *Kabbadi* (game) as shown on the TV. Similarly, my participation in the plays organized by the village youth was helpful in understanding about their interest in other regional languages such as Bhojpuri and Rajasthani.

I was requested by Radha Krishna to plant paddy as demonstrated on the TV during paddy and wheat cultivation. Similarly, the maize planting process was directed by him. In the course of this he often remarked "you have watched on TV very good demonstration, but even then you are not doing it correctly".

The case study method was another technique of collecting data on SITE instructional areas. For this purpose, I selected about twenty villagers in each area of SITE instruction after a month and a half in the village. The subjects were selected from different jatis and economic groups. I conducted an indepth interview to understand their attitudes and knowledge about various issues in pre-SITE period. I also watched them and interviewed them in the during-SITE and post-SITE periods. In this way I could analyse some cases of adoption of innovations shown on the TV. Awareness, interest, knowledge, and adaptation by the target audience in relation to TV programmes could be understood in depth through the case study technique.

To supplement qualitative data, I also applied extended interview techniques. I used schedules for interviewing 20 respondents in during SITE and post-SITE period. As the same respondents were interviewed both the times, I could determine the input of TV programmes to their daily life.

In addition to this, I collected data through a household census and by the genealogical method to understand the size of the family. The genealogical tables of each household yielded important data regarding age, sex, occupation, education etc.

A taperecorder was used in recording group discussions about TV programmes, adoption of songs, and data relevant to linguistic acculturation. In support of the entire body of data on village life, photographs of nearly a hundred situations were taken.

Interaction of the villagers

The Bhumihar and the other higher jatis of the village considered me to be a government spy or an employee of the Central Bureau of Investigation, enquiring about the village factionalism. The Mukhia belonged to one faction, and hence members of the anti-Mukhia faction deterred from speaking to me. However, these inhibitions were broken, when a *Tulsi Manas yajnavas* was held on 18, March 1975 by the anti-Mukhia faction. I got an opportunity to participate in this function. After this, I also participated in the *yajna* and *katha*, held by the villagers. The Bhumihar Brahmins became curious, and asked me many questions—my identity, the purpose of my visit and my affiliation to the department.

During my stay, I became a good friend of Ram Narain Jha, the *Mahapatra* of the village. He accompanied me in the social activities of the village. I had stayed in the village for a week, when Ram Narain requested me to give some guidance to the village youth, who were organizing a play. He said this in one of the rehearsals which I attended with him. I accepted the request and contributed to making a success of the play. After this event, I gained the confidence of the villagers. They became friendly. But unfortunately they had certain fixed opinions . Some of them considered me to be associated with the TV and others considered me to be a social worker, whose main task was to settle the factionalism. Some of them expected me to be involved in their personal and village affair. I was asked to arbitrate in quarrels between two brothers, Rambhusan and Ram Nandan in a dispute over property. I was asked to be a patron in a football match organized by the youth. I had to refuse such requests, since it involved my precious time.

The educated adults, associated with the CPI, took me to be a CIA agent. The CPI leader Thakur spoke to me atleast ten times a week and watched my movements closely. His suspicion continued till the Professor. Sachchidananda visited to the village on 18, October 1975. The other Communist leader also considered me to be a propagandist of the Congress government. This suspicion was intensified when I became friendly with the low jatis and mingled with them, without friendly the social norms.

The CPI leaders considered this to mean a method of propaganda. My refusal to participate in the activities of the CPI organization in the village, which were held twice a week, and my difference of opinion on the theories and ideas of Marx, during discussions were some of the reasons for their suspicion. When I realised this, I made an attempt to say little or nothing on such issues. My attempts were fruitful towards the end of my field work, I became a close friend of Upendra Choudhary, Branch Secretary of the CPI, from whom I obtained relevant data about the political organization and structure of the village.

The lower jatis such as Chamar, Parwan, Mallah and Dhanuk perceived me as a person in charge of distributing ration cards. This was in the initial phase of my field work. In the second phase, they considered me to be a government extension agent. Many of them asked me for government loans for purchasing oxen and buffaloes. The poor people of the village requested for medical aid, to which I replied that I would note down their request in my report, which would be read by the concerned officials. However, I gave some of them the medicines that I carried for personal use.

During the middle phase of my field work, I began noting the viewers' response. This convinced them that I was a TV 'man'. Moreover, my association with the TV personnel who frequently visited the village made the fact obvious.

Children formed an asset in building rapport with the villagers. I participated in their games, *Kamia putra*, *Gulli danda*, and *Ghar ghar*. This appealed to the villagers. Another factor which helped me in building a rapport, was my principle : I always smiled and enquired about a villager's well-being.

Informants

Jaidev Thakur and Ram Narain were my key informants. I met Jaidev Thakur on the third day of my arrival in Barahser.

Thakur was a graduate. He complied to my request, of helping me in conducting a household census. He escorted me to nearby ten houses of Bhumihar Brahmins.

Editorial note

Jha did field work until October 1976. In personal discussion, Jha indicated, that his departure from the field was not very traumatic. In the second week of October, Jha returned to Ahmedabad for analysis of field data.

CHAPTER SIX

THE MOMENTS IN QUIETNESS

by

—ARBIND K. SINHA

Arbind K. Sinha, M.Sc. Anthropology from Ranchi University worked on a number of action projects before joining SITE. After the completion of SITE, he did his Ph.D. using, SITE data. At present, he is a scientist at Space Applications Centre. He was born and brought up in Bihar, in a Hindi speaking family. He was educated in Bihar, Hindi and English being the medium of instruction in school and college.

Anthropologist's house

THE MOMENTS IN QUIETNESS

—ARBIND K. SINHA

ABOUT THE VILLAGE

THE village Ismailpur is situated in Goraul block of Vaishali district in Bihar state, 9 km. from the block headquarters. The first five km from Goraul can be traversed in motor vehicle on tar road while the remaining 4 km. on foot, through a fair weather road. Transport services do not exist beyond Goraul. The post office is located in Sondho, 2 km. south of the village. There is a primary school, health sub-centre, a multi-purpose co-operative society and a non-functioning library in the village. The village comprises of two settlements separated by one-fourth of a kilometre. The main settlement consists of 7 *tolas* (wards) in which the Panchayat Ghar is situated. The village has a population of 1016 of which 84.4 per cent are Hindus and 15.7 per cent are Muslims.

Entering the village

I started my journey from Muzaffarpur on 1, March 1975 and reached Ismailpur within two hours. This was not my first field work and hence not my first exposure to village life. Even then throughout the journey, I felt a certain ease within me and an enthusiasm mingled with perturbed feelings as to what lay ahead.

I reached Goraul by taxi and proceeded from here in a rickshaw to the Block Development Office. When I reached my destination, I found that the Block Development Officer was busy preparing for a Block Development Committee meeting. The Block Development Officer was astonished when he learnt that I was to live in the village Ismailpur for eighteen months.

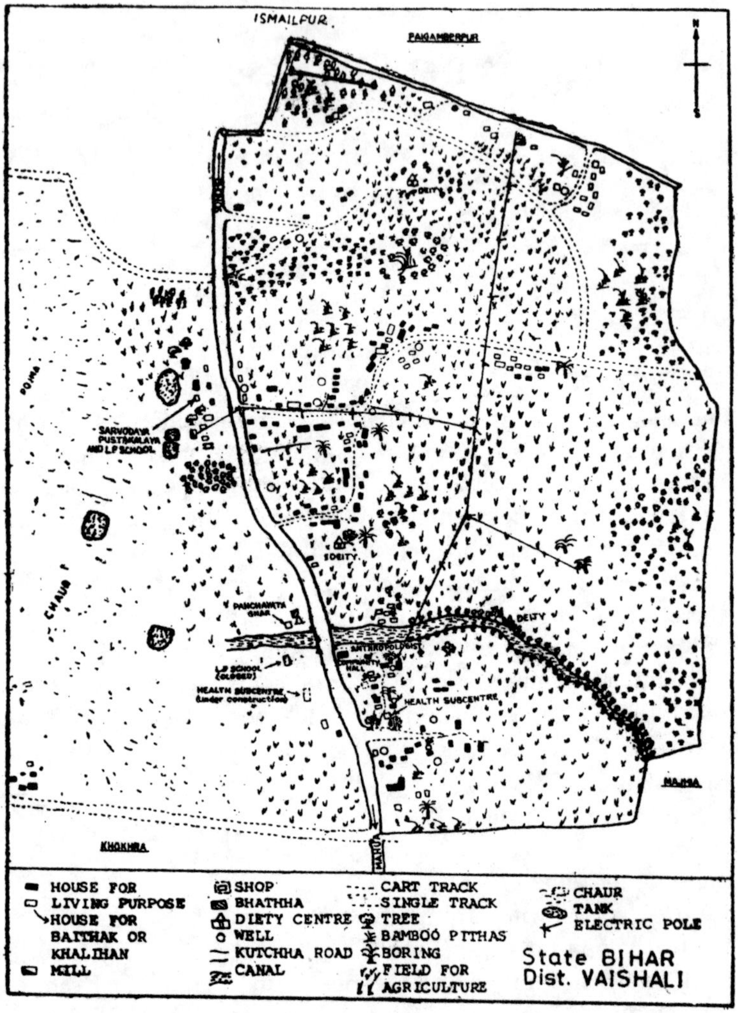

Ismailpur

We had met earlier when I was co-ordinator of the village selection survey*. He said—

*Prior to working on this study, I was involved in the selection of SITE villages for the installation of TV. For this purpose, our team consisting of engineering staff and social scientists visited more than 800 villages in the SITE cluster of Bihar, spanning over a period of eight months.

"You would not be able to live in a village! No, that is not for you. For a person with qualifications and high income such as yours, you need better facilities". He suggested that I stay in the Inspection Bungalow in Goraul and conduct my field work. I explained that this study required my living in the village and that I was, in fact, looking forward to it.

Sure enough, the Block Development Officer had doubts about my long term commitment. He was accustomed to government officials travelling in vehicles accompanied by peons, and he was taken aback by the lack of such paraphernalia. Finally, I proceeded from Goraul in a rickshaw and reached Ismailpur with the help of an escort (person who accompanied me). I began a conversation with him.

"How far is the village ?" to which he replied.
"Not very far. A short distance".
"What is the village like ?"

He looked at me and answered—

"I do not know much for I am new to this place and cannot provide much information" after which we travelled in silence. We reached Sondho weekly market. Here we became friendly with a customer in the fish stall who introduced himself as Hadish. Hadish belonged to the neighbouring village of Ismailpur. He decided to escort us to our destination.

It was a sunny afternoon on the March 1 1976, when I reached Ismailpur. I went to the residence of the *Mukhia* (village council chief) which was situated at one end of the village. The Mukhia was away from Ismailpur and I had to speak with his brother about issues such as boarding and lodging. I requested him to get the community hall cleaned which was being used by the Mukhia as a storage godown for fertilizer sacks. I met Ram Ekwal Singh, the school teacher of Ismailpur. On learning about the purpose of my visit, he immediately complained about the installation of TV in the Panchayat Ghar instead of the school. He claimed "The Mukhia has influence and has thereby installed the TV nearer to his home". Sensing his bitterness I told him that it was the absence of electricity in the school which attributed to this and not any political gains.

By this time, some villagers had recognised me as the engineer sahab of the "village selection survey". They approached me with warmth and friendliness. I proceeded from here to the residence of Hadish of Chainpur, a village situated nearly. Returning to the village from Chainpur, I met the *Panchayat Sewak* (Panchayat clerk) and asked him to meet me the following day with all details of the village Ismailpur, such as statistics pertaining to population.

I reached the Mukhia's house and found that he had returned. I was greeted with a warm welcome. I once again met with a surprised exclamation, when I told him that I would spend eighteen months in the village. He required :

> "Are you from the State or Central Government ?"
> What is your designation and salary ? What is your job?"

These were important questions obviously to the Mukhia. He seemed pleased with what I had to tell him. He then began narrating incidents indicating his influence and power and his contribution to the village welfare.

After having rested for a night, the morning awake me to the beginning of my task. I asked the Mukhia to clear the fertilizer sacks which were stored in the hall and make room for my living. He did so after two days. With the help of a servant, I cleaned the room and burnt *Humadh** to remove the smell of the fertilizer. I also purchased a stove and started cooking my meals in a pressure cooker. Thus, I began my first few days in Ismailpur.

In my initial acquaintance, I met with some hostility from the villagers for a rumour had spread that I was from the CBI (Central Bureau of Investigation). Still others treated me as a doctor sahab, for the village doctor had previously resided here. And some of them thought that I was a Village Level Worker. In short, I was a stranger and the villagers were not clear about my purpose of visit. This then was my beginning.

For the first six months, I lived in a room in the community

**Humadh*—inferior quality sandalwood chips—incense.

hall. I spent the first ten days with the stink of the fertilizer that had been stored in the room. Burning Humadh every day was little help and it was only after ten days that the place became habitable. This room opened towards the north and also had windows facing north wards and south wards. It provided a good view of the pace and activity of village life and I could spend hours observing the stream of activity from my window.

In June 1975 Shyamnandan, one of the key informants of the village moved into my residence and lived here till the end of field work. We built a good rapport.

In mid-September 1975, I felt that it was necessary to have the house electrified and hence invested an amount of Rs. 400/ to do so. I also requested the Mukhia for more living space in the community hall. By the beginning of October, I managed to acquire the adjacent room. Now, I had a fairly good semi-pucca house (brick walls and tiled roof) with a kitchen, latrine, verandah, courtyard and two rooms.

The location of the community hall was at a strategic spot, in the south of the village near the panchayat ghar. It was a central point joining Dhuntoli and southern ward. A canal which flowed nearby was filled with water during the months of July to February and afforded many quite hours of aloneness, when I would sit on the culvert, looking deep into the waters in contemplative silence. This was also a meeting place for the villagers and many evenings were spent getting together and talking into the night. The village of course slept easily.

My family visited me for twenty seven days* which was a welcome change. However, on 24, February 1976, a veternary doctor, (Block Animal Husbandary Officer) posted in the area decided to reside in the community hall with his family. Hence, I once again shifted into my one room to stay until 8, October 1976.

Jati and self-identity

I introduced myself—

"I am Arbind Sinha from Patna district. I work for

*I was married while working on this project and at this time, my family included my wife.

the Television Department in Ahmedabad and I am here to conduct a study".

This of course was the gist of what I often repeated while meeting many villagers. But the inevitable question that I was faced with was—

"What is your jati?"

To which I replied that I belonged to the Kurmi jati. The numerically dominant jati in Ismailpur were the Awadhiya who were an endogamous group of Kurmi jati. My jati identity was a major factor in providing crucial linkages with the villagers affecting various issues and relationships.

Many old men (old men were respected and claimed authority) commented— "This educated young gentleman belongs to our jati. We have to be good to him and provide him with all that he wants. Or else he would report back to his home town in Patna District about our lack of hospitality. I was often referred to as a *hakim*, a word used to connote respect and addressed to the panchayat sewak, Village Level Worker, (VLW) teacher, compounder, doctor, Block Development Officer and District Magistrate.

I soon became accepted as a member of the Awadhiya jati. So much so, that I was asked to arbitrate in household and village disputes, from which I had to tactfully withdraw. A strong feeling lingered among villagers that I could be a "resource person" in terms of marriage alliances across Patna and Ismailpur. I was asked to negotiate in marriage alliances within the village.

Many villagers were of the opinion that I would be a model for the youth and be appraised by the literate old folk. But to the contrary, many old rich cultivators complained of my intermingling with the Harijans and this was not appealing especially when some of the Awadhiya youth accompanied me to mingle with the Harijans.

In fact, my presense and behaviour created tension. On the one hand, the Harijans were pleased and demanded that they be treated with dignity by members of Awadhiya jati, while the Awadhiya insisted that I lay my boundaries and follow the existing norms of my jati in interrelating with the Harijans. The jarring note was that, in my anthropological field study, my enquiry about norms, social customs and taboos to the Awadhiya were often retorted back with the statement,

"You know all about it. Why are you asking us?" Hence with expectations and demands meted to me, I had to take a stance in every context and situation and deal with the people in a tactful manner.

Living a day in Ismailpur

Life begins early in Ismailpur. But my hours of working were unrestricted and dependent on the late hours of the previous night. Each day followed another with a similar pattern of events and routine, broken now and then by visits to the villagers' homes, and receiving guests. The morning began with a stroll into the street observing the beginning of the day's activities, stopping by to converse with people. I would proceed to the canal for a wash. Gazing into the water, watching the fishes, talking to villagers, collecting data and information in these moments were all part of the morning chores. I would then visit selected informants, sometimes walking for long distances in order to do so. At about 11'Oclock, I would return home to prepare a meal and dine either alone or in the company of the visitors. They would relax comfortably, chewing tobacco and occasionally fetching a glass of water from my pitcher. And so we would chat through the afternoon. At times, this routine was broken when I was invited for lunch on special occasions in the household, or on festivals.

I spent the evenings in the Panchayat Ghar. Occasionally, I would accompany an informant to the neighbouring villages. When the dusk fell, crassing the sense of remoteness in me, casting a mystic reverse upon the canal, I would walk over to sit near the mill of Shyamnandan Sahu or under the banyan tree. Or else, I would visit a villager's house to collect information. After returning, I would prepare my meals and then spend the rest of the evening with the village youth, conversing and gossiping before returning for the night.

This then was my daily routine in the pre-SITE stage. With the beginning of SITE, I spent the mornings and evenings watching TV and noting the response of the viewers. After transmission I would return to my room. The late hours of the night were spent in the company of the cultivators and the youth. Finally, before returning after an exhausted day, I noted down the day's events in my diary. During summer, in the months of May, June and July, I avoided walking in the sun specially in the peak hours of heat between 11 a.m. and 4 p.m. Living a day in Ismailpur can be uneventful. Yet' I found new avenues of learning in my day to day experience.

Constraints or challenge ?

Familiarity with the constraints and difficulties in a village provides a self-assurance. Yet, situations vary, calling for new adjustments, adaptations and decisions.

One such incident which posed conflicts and demanded tact and coping strategy was with regard to the cultural activities of the village. I was asked to take charge of the direction and supervision of a play, which had overtones of anti-government messages and criticism of its administration. This was the time when all such demonstrations and activities were being curbed by the government, for Emergency had been declared in the country. I was faced with a delicate situation. If I conceded to the request of the villagers, I would be reported by the police to the higher authority and if I did not, I would be considered by the villagers as a mere government official, unconcerned with their welfare. Finally, with the assistance of a school teacher, I managed to convince the villagers about the irrelevance of certain parts of the play. I took charge of the direction and staged the play with modifications.

Lack of water resources within reach of my living quarters was a constraint. According to the original construction plan of the community hall, a hand pump was scheduled to be installed which was overlooked. I approached the Block Development Officer about this issue who informed the council chief to pursue the matter. Finally, a hand pump was installed with 20 feet depth in boring instead of 60 feet, which provided sandy water, unhealthy for consumption. So much so, that my maid servant had to fetch drinking water from the council chief's house after waiting for long hours. She was also forced to do odd jobs for him in return for the drinking water provided to me.

Another issue which bothered me was the impingement of my privacy by the unemployed youth. With the day's end, they would accompany me home after transmission and spend late hours talking into the night, having little time to pounder or reflect on the day's events or to be with myself. These are issues that one is familiar within a village, and has no choice except to deal with them as best as one can.

Visitors

One welcomes friends and relatives while living in a village, for the contact with the outside world is replenishing. I had many visitors—my supervisors from Ahmedabad who came for supervision and checking of TV materials, research fellows and research assistants from SITE and A.N. Sinha Institute of Social Studies, the Block Development Officer as well as other local officials.

It was a hot April after noon when Dr. Binod C. Agrawal project leader came in an *ekka* (horse cart) down the streets of Ismailpur. It sure enough, created a stir in the village. He walked up to me, and we greeted each other as relatives. But the villagers were shrewd to sense that he was an official while hearing our discussion on issues such as the concept of jati. Almost every visitor from the city was introduced as a friend or a relative except for Prof. Yash Pal, Director of Space Applications Centre, Ahmedabad whose arrival was planned and announced.

My role as an anthropologist

Impression management is tried by the investigator at times and very often he has to play significant roles. His role includes living as a villager, speaking the language and adapting to the norms and customs of the village life. I succeeded in doing this.

Yet my role did not end here. My involvement in the life of the villagers led to personalization of relationships. One of the main factors that provided crucial linkages with the villagers was my jati affiliation. I was accepted as a member of the numerically dominant Awadhiya jati of the village and given an important status for my education and income. Hence, I was often asked to play the role of an adviser and negotiator in marriage alliances. I was often addressed—

> "We would feel honoured and be given an important status by the groom's party if you would accompany us".

I refused their request stating

> "The old men are wise and experienced and I am inefficient in these matters. You should ask them".

On one such instance I was asked to convince the groom about the legitimate beauty and talents of the bride. I told him,

> "You should rely on your own convictions and not listen to others opinions in making your decision".

There were instances where my role as a mediator between the marriage parties was successful, as in the Teli jati household. When asked to negotiate in the fixing of cattle price between two parties, I refrained from doing so, stating my inefficiency and ignorance in dealing with such matters.

Shyamnandan of Ismailpur and Ramasheesh of Majhia were two of my close associates whom I considered as intelligent and hard working. Hence, I suggested their names for training in an agricultural training programme as well as a development programme. I also helped Ramasheesh in purchasing a motor cycle and a tractor and taught him driving.

Role of government officials

The authenticity and commitment of government officials towards village welfare seemed negligible. On my part, I refrained to act on behalf of the villagers, for I considered myself incapable. The villagers encountered many difficulties. For instance, in the installation of the hand pump, the whole matter had to be pursued with insistence. I also encountered many constraints in dealing with the government officials. In my attempt to acquire information on co-operative functioning in the village, the block development officials were unwilling to render help, and finally I had to approach the district level officials. These are instances which illustrate the varying situations and circumstances that I encountered and the ways in which I dealt with them.

The last days in Ismailpur

I had informed the villagers that I would depart from Ismailpur after the *Durga puja.* The news about my departure on 10 October, 1976 soon spread within an hour on 3 October, 1976, when I received the letter to report back to Ahmedabad. While collecting data for supplementary survey, I was met with the question "Are you really leaving us ?" The young women who never spoke directly to me enquired about my departure through the older women, and some of them enquired if this was merely a short visit and if I would return to Ismailpur.

I had invitations for lunch and dinner every day and the Block Animal Husbandry Officer offered breakfast in the mornings.

My maid servant wept bitterly expressing her sentiments and grief. Her income of Rs. 40 earned from the Block Animal Husbandry Officer and me had substantiated her living. Shyamnandan could not continue to live in the community hall. The electricity connection was to be cut after my departure. These disadvantages were disturbing to the Block Animal Husbandry Officer and Shyamnandan.

I visited the residence of the council chief. I was greeted by his brother. He expressed his grief. I was informed that the council chief was glad that I was leaving, for my presence had been a constraint—the bitterness and anger expressed against the council chief by the poor could not be curbed due to my presence. The children were least affected by my departure and it was only while packing that one of them exclaimed with a forlorn face "Oh! he's really going".

"It is unfair that you should be cooking meals in the last few days" was a remark of an old man, who touching me by the arm invited me to his home. Women applauded praise—"He is a good man. His heart is big. He helped everyone without partiality." Some of the villagers offered land and requested me to build a house and settle down in Ismailpur.

Many old women complained "you are leaving us and we have not seen your son.* The women of Dhuntoli were touched

*By this time I was blessed with a son. My wife and child were living with my father.

with my affection. "He is so good to the poor and probably the Mukhia did not want him and has therefore issued a transfer".

On 4, October 1976, when the dawn had set and the sun was yet to rise, I was awakened by a knock at the door. I opened, to find a villager standing with a jug of milk. He requested me to take it since I was leaving and insisted that I continue to take his milk for the next few days. I refused stating "I have my usual supply of milk for which I pay. So I do not want this. Instead I will join you for dinner".

On the 5th night, many villagers came over to enquire "When are you leaving ?" "Will you come back ?" "How are you travelling ?" "Where is your destination ?" and "Can we have your address ?" The school teacher told me that he would write to Mrs. Gandhi* requesting for extension of my stay and obtain the signatures of the villagers for the purpose. On the 7th, I strolled through the village, meeting the villagers. I had to wade through water which caused infection and swelling in my legs. In the night, my legs ached and I lay awake. Shyamnandan remained tossing and turning in bed and I felt tears in my eyes, sensing his affection and pain.

I gave a gift of Rs. 10 to my servant who began weeping and said "Never before in my life time did I receive so much respect from the villagers. Nobody dared to tease me in your presence. The villagers, referring to the community hall said, *chaman ujad jayega* (the garden will turn into a desert.)

The jeep scheduled to arrive at 8 O' clock came at 11.30 a.m. on the 8th. In the morning I received crafts, garlands and gifts from the villagers. They gathered in my room and wished a formal goodbye. Finally the jeep moved through the streets of the village while the villagers waved their last goodbye. The thought flashed through my mind "So lovely, warm and tender a people who give so much and for whom I have nothing to offer. This then is the end of another phase of my career. How long do I have to go and how much can I do ?"

*The then Prime Minister of India.

CHAPTER SEVEN

THE GOOD OFFICIAL

J.B. AMBEKAR

J.B. Ambekar joined this project after completing his M.A. in Anthropology from Dharwad University. He completed his Ph.D. using SITE data and joined Deptt. of Sociology Shivaji University, Kolhapur, Maharashtra.

He was born in a Kannada speaking urban town of Karnataka in a Marathi speaking household. He was educated in Karnataka, Kannada/English being the medium of instruction in school and college.

THE GOOD OFFICIAL

—J.B. AMBEKAR

ABOUT THE VILLAGE

THE VILLAGE Pothnal is 21 km from its taluka headquarters Manvi and 70 km from its district headquarters Raichur, considered as one of the underdeveloped districts in Karnataka state. Express and ordinary buses traversing the route between Raichur and Hubli halt at Pothnal. There is no railway route connecting Pothnal to towns and cities. However, the village is situated on the state highway, with a frequency of buses every half an hour during the day. Further, Pothnal is centrally located.

I have described in this account, my interaction with the villagers of Pothnal, the process of my transactions and communication with them and the role that I played as an anthropologist; life in Pothnal as I lived and experienced during my field work, merging work and social life; the impact that I left behind, and the significant relationships built with some of the villagers whose warmth and friendliness characteristic of the traditions of rural North Karnataka that I cherish; I have stated all this and more.

Entering the village

I reached Pothnal on 15, July 1975* My first meeting was

*J.B. Ambekar replaced M. Jahagirdar who initially conducted this study. He found himself incapacitated to live in a village for field work. Hence, after consultation and personal discussion, it was felt that J.B. Ambekar would replace Jahagirdar. In the process, two and a half months had lapsed from the schedule of the launching of the study.

J.B. Ambekar missed the initial training given to the other anthropologists. But, he went through the discussion held for two weeks and who read specific material prepared for this study.

with the peon of the co-operative society who informed me about the whereabouts of the Gowda (headman) of the village. He described him as a person with a good heart, helpful and co-operative, economically stable and owning many houses. I was soon to find that almost everyone in the village considered him in the same light. It led me to wonder if this person was an influential and benevolent political leader of the village.

In my initial meeting with the Gowda, he stated "Television is not important for the poor. It is only for government servants and people from affluent sections of society". The Gowda continued this stance throughout the field work. He did not attend the TV programmes. After my initial meeting, my interactions with him were limited to a few instances. However, I became friendly with his brother who was sociable and played cards and games with the village youth, having little work to do.

My home in Pothnal

Initially, I stayed in the main part of the village for three

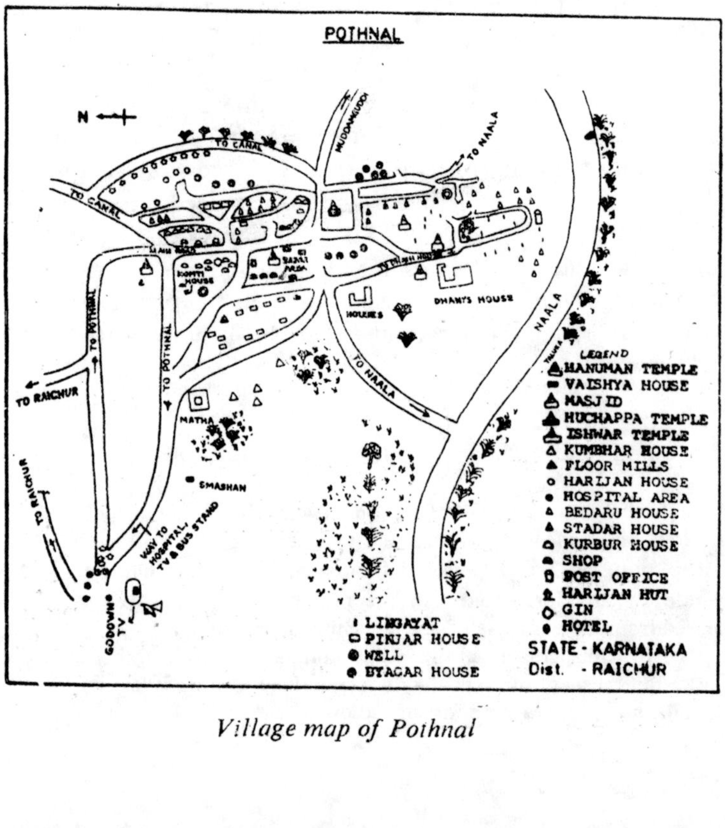

Village map of Pothnal

months. I later shifted about 200 meters away from the main settlement into the outskirts. Subbaraju, an ayurvedic doctor from Andhra Pradesh and his young daughter Ram Seeta helped in providing me with a hut. From the very beginning I was indentified as a good government servant, associated with the TV. So when I shifted to my second home, which was in the neighbourhood of the government officials, I was identified with them. Such a situation, insulated me from active day to day interaction with the shopkeepers whose shops were situated near the busstand and with the villagers who visited Subbaraju the ayurvedic doctor. However, the presence of my grand mother, who was staying with me increased my interaction with the women.

Interaction with villagers

My association with the villagers began with the commencement of the survey of household census.* During the survey, I spoke to them about agriculture, family planning, television and other aspects concerning their welfare. I learnt their opinion on technological innovation in agriculture. The geneological charts helped me to understand about the status, roles and relationships of the household members. I stated about my purpose of visit. "I am here, working for Television experiment. I would like to learn about your reactions and preferences about the TV programmes". My friendly approach soon found acknowledgement among many of the villagers. I was accepted as a friend.

My grandmother lived with me during my field work. Her presence was not only reassuring in terms of providing emotional anchorage but also in her playing the significant role

*I had a distinct disadvantage over other anthropologists who were conducting similar field studies, as I was late to begin my field work by two and half months. I was also deprived of the initial discussion on the theoritical assumptions and understanding of communication process in which others had participated. I was asked to work on this project while I was in field, as a member of SITE survey team. I went to Ahmedabad and after the initial two week special training and discussions returned to Pothnal for field work. In one way, I felt very fortunate that I did not have to carry the image of the earlier anthropologist, who had not spent anytime in the field beyond one or two nights.

of a 'resource person' in building linkages with the villagers. She looked after household matters such as cooking and cleaning which gave me ample time for field work. Many village women would visit our home and spend long hours chatting with us. I found this to be a constraint at times since I could never allot time for my field notes.

Nevertheless, my grandmother always had time for the village women and had discussions on matters such as child rearing practices of the village, food habits, language and dress of the villagers. So much so, that she learnt a lot about many aspects of village life. The information which she provided enriched my data. She was also helpful in searching notes and files that I needed for reference or for writing notes (she had received minimum education and had, in her youth worked in a hospital during the British regime). Her presence gave me a sense of belonging in the village.

Living a day in Pothnal

As my field work had started only a few weeks prior to SITE which began on 1, August 1975, my field work in its real sense began during the SITE year. In July, the first two weeks were concentrated on collecting census data and in drawing the village map. Hence, my description of a day in Pothnal basically follows the pattern that I had maintained during SITE year. My primary focus on viewing the morning and evening telecast defined the daily routine. Every morning I would walk through the village streets talking to children and whomever I met. In order to organise my field work, I identified one household in each street of the village with whom I established close ties. I would sit in their homes and collect information of the events and activities that might have occurred during the preceding day or in my absence.

Then, from the village, I would start back to TV centre before 10'O clock, located in the co-operative society building (away from the village and the school). I would participate in viewing the childrens' programme telecast from 10 a.m. to 10.30 a.m. on all days of the week except holidays and return to the village. Again in the evenings I would go to the village at about 4'O clock and spend about two hours returning to attend the TV programmes at 6.30 p.m. I watched TV and observed the viewers' reaction to the programme. I stayed here till 9 p.m.

My field work included getting details of the audience response to the programme. Thus, in my queries as to how much of the details the farmers assimilated from the programmes and how clear they were about the information they would reply, saying—

> "It is you who show us the programmes and why do you ask us such questions? Why do you test our memory ?"

In spite of such questions, I would pursue them to give their opinion on the programmes.

I visited the homes of informants from whom I received information on methods of cultivation when we talked about various aspects of village life and domestic issues. The field work thus brought close ties between the villagers and me and I could obtain information on almost any issue for they did not hesitate to provide details to my queries. My close friends helped me in cross checking my observations and recording the field notes. I was treated with respect and dignity and received well. So much so that our friendship drew us together often for tea and lunch in our homes.

I attended *bhajans*, fairs and festivals. I would take my recorder with me on these occasions and it was always received with delight and enthusiasm. Recording the bhajans and songs and replaying it, brought joy and happiness to the villagers. Neither did they hesitate in talking about various issues while I recorded the conversation. Very often, when I took photographs, I was asked if I would be sending them for display in TV.

Government officials in Pothnal

A part of the SITE experiment included the involvement of State Government officials, belonging to the Block Development Office, Education department, Primary Health Centres, and other such departments. There were twenty government officials residing in Pothnal. Often the Village Level Workers (VLW), compounder, agricultural extension officers and school teachers approached me to help them fill the forms supplied by the government departments and National Council for Education Research and Training. I helped them since I needed their assistance for obtaining information on several issues. Hence, I could establish a rapport with them. When asked about their work input in Pothnal, many of the government officials confessed about their negligence in work.

Post-SITE field work

The TV transmission ended on 31, July 1976, which created a void in the lives of the villagers, amply described by the youth who would sit idly on the steps of the village temple, stating—

> "Oh! When TV was here, we had something to occupy our time. Now it is so difficult to pass time since there is nothing to do."

I experienced a similar situation, since I had to modify my daily routine of field work. I began noting the reactions and responses of the villagers about their feelings towards closing of TV transmission. A week after the end of TV transmission I found to my surprise and delight that many of the children could remember the school songs and the names of animals displayed on the TV screen. Some of them even tried their hands successfully in making dolls after watching the programmes.

In the beginning of August, when the villagers learnt of my approaching departure from Pothnal, they enquired, "Are you shifting the TV to other villages ? Why are you taking the set ? When will you come again to the village ? Where are you going ? When will you be employed ? What work will you do?" The villagers asked these questions often during the post. SITE phase.

Some of the farmers were very friendly and close to me and I could obtain any information that I needed. I considered them as my key informants. In fact, the bonds were such that I often forgot my task, as that of interviewing them. I would yield in informal discussions about customs, food habits of a particular jati, and other such issues.

Departing from Pothnal

When I finally conveyed the news of my departure from

Pothnal, two weeks preceding the date of departure, the cultivators broke down in tears saying "We do not know, when we would be able to meet you again. Are you going to return to Pothnal ?" They conversed amongst themselves. "He was a good man. He treated every villager alike, irrespective of his wealth or poverty."

I had during the course of my field work, become very friendly with the villagers. The camera and the tape recorder helped in establishing a rapport with the men and children and to a small extent, with the women. It dawned on me, that my departure from Pothnal would be painful for the personalization of relationships and the sense of belonging that I experienced, that were being severed would be hard to cope with. I also felt the affection of the villagers who asked me to stay in Pothnal, saying that life would be more expensive outside. Many of the villagers expressed their grief and many discussed the issue of my departure.

During the last three or four days of my stay in Pothnal, my discussions with the informants always centred on the issue of my departure. Impact survey T_2 had begun by this time, and hence I was busy in my field work. My informants, with a forlorn look in their eyes stated "Who knows whether we would see his face again?" They helped me in packing my luggage and shifting it to the bus stop. When I reached the bus stop, I found a crowd of people waiting to bid me a farewell. Amidst the chatter, tears, melancholy and sorrow, I boarded the bus when it reached the bus stand. I wave to the arms that waved. And as the bus moved, I saw the crowd thinning to be replaced by trees, bushes and fields.

CHAPTER EIGHT

A LIE CAN BE A HALF-TRUTH

RAVI P. RAI

Ravi P. Rai took his M.A. (Anthropology) from Lucknow University. He began working on this project after an initial attempt in Audience Research. After completion of SITE he joined the Indian Institute of Management, Ahmedabad to work on a similar Research Project.

Ravi Rai was born and brought up in a Bhojpuri speaking family of Uttar Pradesh. He was educated in Lucknow where his medium of instruction was Hindi and English.

Interviewing villagers

A LIE CAN BE A HALF-TRUTH

—RAVI P. RAI

ABOUT THE VILLAGE

The state of Rajasthan is divided into twenty six districts. Sawai Madhopur is one of the districts situated on the eastern border of Rajasthan. The village Khedli is located in the western part of Sawai Madhopur district. Jaipur is 121 km from Khedli. It is not an isolated village as it is situated on the Jaipur-Gangapur road. The village is accessible throughout the year and every half an hour the bus passes through the village. Population of the revenue village of Khedli is 1357, according to 1971 Census.

The first visit to Khedli

I visited the village Khedli on 1, October 1975* While approa-

*Initially, village Khedli was selected for field work by Dr. J.K. Doshi who had visited the village in early 1975. As there was no Anthropology Department in Rajasthan, it became an extremely difficult task to search for an Anthropologist who could conduct field work in Khedli. Hence, the study was to be abandoned. As a last effort, Ravi Rai and his wife Kumkum Rai were selected to conduct the field work two months after the SITE had started. Due to technical faults, TV in Khedli could not become operational until October. The arrival of the Anthropologists coincided with the operation of the TV. Initially, Kumkum Rai was inducted in the field work to compensate the loss of time as scheduled. It was observed by the Project Leader and other members of the Research Team that a special study on women vis-a-vis TV for development and Education would be of great interest. This led to the decision of entrusting Kumkum Rai to conduct a fullfledged study on TV and women. The basic data had been shared by Ravi and Kumkum Rai whereas special data on women was collected by Kumkum Rai. From the following description it will be clear that Kumkum Rai maintained the role of a housewife throughtout her field work whereas Ravi Rai was viewed by the villagers as an anthropologist in the field.

ching the village in a jeep, I could see the antenna of the TV silhoutted against the deep blue sky even from a distance. On reaching the village, I was welcomed by the school teachers and the young men of the village who had seen the jeep approaching. I introduced myself to the school teachers. The TV was installed in the school building. I visited the school premises with the school teachers. I then told them that I would be living in Khedli for a year. The assistant teacher and custodian, quietly, and in what seemed to me, conspicuously, took me aside to enquire about my jati. I told him that I was a Brahmin and he was pleased.

Dr. J.K. Doshi, Co-Project Leader had informed me about Ram Swaroop Gupta whom he had said, would be helpful in arranging for my accommodation. I also contacted Suresh, son

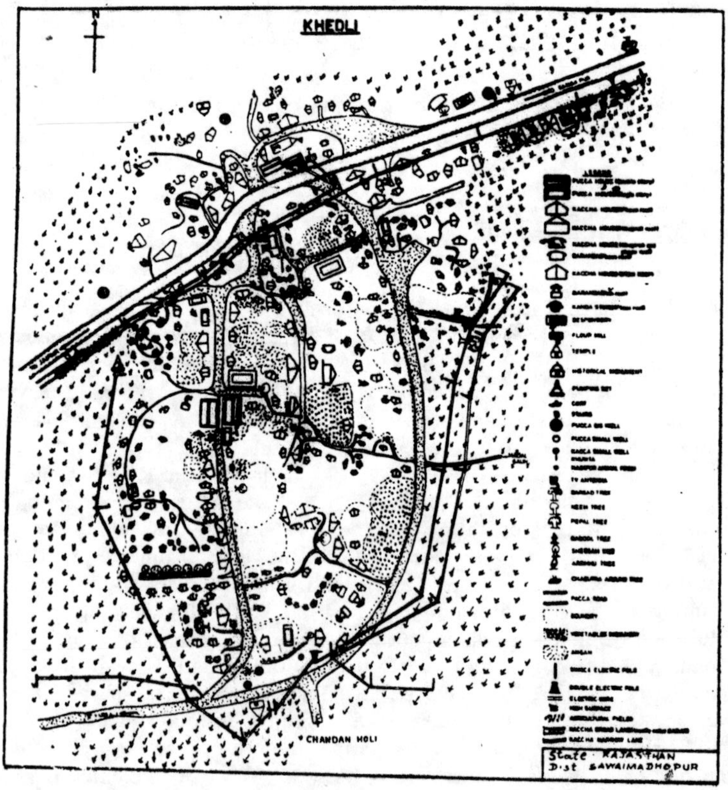

Village map of Khedli

of Radhey Shyam Sharma, a wealthy villager who assured his help in providing a portion of his house to accommodate us. Many villagers enquired about my jati and I was surprised to find that they were pleased with my answer. I left Khedli with a feeling of satisfaction for having raised the issue of my accommodation.

Entering the village

My second visit was scheduled for beginning my field work and to stay in Khedli for a year. My wife Kumkum accompanied me, and we reached Khedli on 22, October 1975 at 10 a.m. The bus stopped in front of the school building. We entered the school, and met the primary school teachers. After the formal introduction, they informed us that they were attending the Science Teachers Training course along with twelve other teachers. I enquired about Suresh to learn that he had left for Gangapur. Instead, we met his uncle (father's younger brother) who led the way to his house, to show us the room we were to stay. The rent was Rs. 25 excluding the electricity charges. The teacher on learning about it, said that the rent was exorbitant and asked Ram Swaroop to accompany me to find a better accommodation. While discussing the rent my wife went along with a village girl, who requested her to visit her home.

I finally settled for a pucca house situated in the centre of the village. I visited the premises. The accommodation consisted of two rooms in the first floor, bigger in size to the one we had seen previously. Situated in the centre of the village, the house provided a good view of the ebb and flow of village life. On the ground floor was a grocery shop, which the villagers often visited. The neighbourhood was a multi-jati locality, and except for Sanjoge Vaïshnava jati, the other jati households were situated here.

After settling about the accommodation, the school teacher and I began walking towards the school. He stopped on the way to join some villagers smoking *ganja** in *chilams*** in front of a pan shop. The school teacher introduced me and left me to make friends with my new acqaintances. One of

* Ganja—Marijuana

**Chilams—pipe used for smoking marijuana

them asked me—

> "Sahib, will you take our photographs and display it on TV ?" to which I replied.

> "No, brother I do not take photographs. My task is to live with you in the village, watch TV programmes, observe your reactions and responses, your understanding, your conception of its utility—in short find out what TV has meant to you ?"

An old man then turned to me and enquired

> "To which jati do you belong ?" I told him that I was a Brahmin. He replied

> "Maharaj, God bless you ; Be happy ; Stay with us as long as you wish."

It had started to drizzle. The men dispersed slowly. I learnt later, that they belonged to the Gujjar jati.

I went to the school where I joined my wife. The school teachers on training enquired, "Will we get any allowance or remuneration for the training." I told them that I was ignorant about such issues. It continued to rain. Electricity had been cut and hence TV transmission was cancelled. My wife and I had nothing else to do except board a bus to Gangapur.

We returned to Khedli with out luggage the next morning at 10.30 a.m. Leaving my wife to unpack in our new home, I went to a well near my home along with my house owner and a brahmin youth, Sitaram. I saw three women bathing beside the well after which they entered the temple close by and paid homage to the idol with their palms folded in prayer. Touched with the sense of serenity and antiqueness, I expressed my respect for the women to my companion. I then proceeded with Sitaram to his home. Sitaram consented to help in household errands for a monthly payment of Rs 40. I began to settle down in the village. Living in the village was demanding, calling for adjustments and arrangements and presenting myself in a manner that was appealing to the villagers.

Within a day or so of settling in my home, my landlord expressed his anxieties, for his elder brother suspected me to be a government employee, reporting about the corruption in the village. He also stated that he would keep his commitment to me, with regard to my accommodation and face whatever consequences he may have to meet. However, within a few days of my stay, these suspicions and fears were forgotten, for they were convinced by my attitude and behaviour that my work was not what they suspected.

The second occasion when I had to prove my integrity was when I filled in the attendance sheet during TV viewing in the evening. This caused the Gujjar men to suspect that I would ask them to pay a tax. I met them the following day to explain the purpose of my data collection. The third occasion was in my field work, while collecting background data for Tı SITE Impact Survey Schedule. I questioned the respondents about the income expenditure and land holdings which created suspicions in their minds about my role and task. "Why do you ask such intimate questions ? What relevance do these questions have to TV programme ?" It was difficult to explain and prove my authenticity. They were finally convinced when I pointed out that if this were to be a matter for secrecy, I could have obtained the records from the *patwari* instead of asking them. This approach and answer however made my field work easier in the days to come.

If suspicions and fears arose, doubting my credentials and status, this was only on specific occasions for instance, when I questioned them about their personal lives. However, the villagers had a fond affection for me, which they expressed often.

> "We have never seen a government servant who could be so gentle......He speaks to all and sundry relates to children as a child, and to elders with respect and politeness . . ."

Identity and jati

Hindus and Jains were dominant in the village. Since I was a Hindu Brahmin, I was accepted by the villagers. I performed and observed the rites and fasts on festivals and religious occasions. I visited the temple shrines. These activities made me a part of the village, and gave me a sense of belonging. I was respected by members of the lower jatis as well as the higher jatis. However, a few men of the Gujjar jati asked me to spend less time with members of the lower jati. On one occasion when invited for dinner to a Gujjar household, I was told that my dinner was cooked by a Brahmin in order to avoid ritual pollution. I then explained that jati discrimination was not important and the family seemed to be pleased.

Informants

Though my attempt was to be friendly with every villager, I however established a close rapport with a few villagers. My friends did not belong to one single jati or age group, but were varied and the disparity in their economic status was also significant. Radhey Shyam Sharma, a graduate holding a B.Ed., degree was unemployed. He helped his father in agricultural activities, assisted him in running the shop and helped his younger brother, with school work. He was religious and pious, with sincere affections to his beloved, who was employed in a hospital. I considered his character to be flawless. He accompanied me to the various households of the village.

My home in Khedli

My wife and I resided in the first floor, occupying two rooms while the landlord's youngest brother stayed in the third one. In the ground floor, there were three shops owned by the three Dayal brothers. The youngest brother transacted money lending, and hence whenever the shop was closed, the villagers visited him in his room. Since the house was situated in a multi-jati locality, we found an access to meeting villagers of different jati frequently.

Visitors

My in-laws, who included my brother-in-law (wife's brother) mother-in-law and sister-in-law visited our home in Khedli. My brother-in-law was fun loving and was gifted with a good sense of humour. The villagers found him entertaining and he soon won their appreciation and goodwill. The villagers became very fond of my relatives who were equally impressed by their warmth and friendliness.

Living a day in Khedli

My day would begin at around 6' O clock in the morning.

After the morning chores and breakfast which took about an hour or so I would begin my field work. My work included observing the villagers and interviewing them. At 10.15 a.m, I would walk down to the school, to watch TV, talk to school teachers and interview students. Then I would once again conduct my field work in the evening at about 4.00 p.m. I would visit the village market observing and noting down events and episodes of village life and interview the villagers. At about 6.45 p.m. I would attend the evening TV programme and converse to TV viewers. The evening was spent speaking to TV viewers and attending to other official work. This then was my daily schedule.

However, I encountered some constraints which were detrimental to the daily schedule. One such constraint was the arrival of guests at late hours of the night. The villagers would get together at my home. In their enthusiasm to learn more about me and discuss and talk about many issues, they would sit many hours, at times even till early morning, which upset my routine for the day. The guests included the school teacher and village officials.

The daily schedule was at times disturbed by events and activities such as *Panchayat Gramasamaj** and such informal meetings, festivals, marriages, deaths and receiving officials from outside the village. Occasionally, I had to leave Khedli to visit Gangapur, Jaipur and Ahmedabad for research work. At times, the TV transmission would be delayed or cancelled due to failure of electricity or during the rainy season when the villagers found it impossible to attend the programme.

P.C. Jain owned a shop at Riplani, two kilometres away from Khedli. He later found employment at Raisa, 55 km from Khedli. The middle aged Guptaji had a shop where villagers from different parts of the village met and assembled to discuss various issues and subjects. K. Mal was young Mali who was a member of *Nav Yuvak Mandal* (Youth Organization) helped me in collecting data from his jati members, and proved himself to be a good informant and friend.

Khandelwal was my wife's ritual brother and became an object for jokes and talk of the village. Several members of Koli and Gujjar jati were good friends and reliable informants.

*Village Society.

Jain Sharma, M. Jain, S.M. Sharma and K.S. Mahajan were other friends and informants.*

Departure from Khedli

In late September, I broke the news that I would be departing from Khedli very soon, for I had to reach Ahmedabad by 11, October 1976. The date of my departure had been scheduled for October 5.

On hearing about my departure, one of the villagers sent a letter to Ahmedabad, requesting for our permanent stay in Khedli, with signatures from the villagers and a seal from the *sarpanch* (village headman). I had to explain that such a request would not be consented. On a late evening, the president of the co-operative society of the village beckoned me while I was talking to the villagers, and taking me aside stated—

> "The villagers are willing to contribute up to Rs. 4000 to revoke your transfer". I replied

> "I appreciate and respect your feelings. I thank you for your kindness and affection. But no one can stop me from leaving since this is essential."

Many of the villagers expressed their grief—

> "You are departing, only to leave behind you a deadening silence."

One of them recited a couplet—

> "Strangers love as of a straw,
> and departing, leaves survival to them."

In the days preceding my departure, my wife and I visited the villagers' homes for dinner and lunch. They helped me to pack my belongings. On 5, October 1976, 25 villagers, remained at my residence, chatting through the night. On 6, October 1976 I was to leave in the morning for Jaipur. Many of the

*Some of the names have been changed in order to maintain anonymity.

villagers assembled and we had tea together. After this, I visited the villagers' homes, where I was served tea and food. Then, in an open verandah, at the central market place, my wife and I were seated on a carpet and garlanded while the Pandit chanted hymns and placed *tikka* on our foreheads. We were offered Rs. 101 which we declined and instead accepted Rs. 11 on their insistence, since this was a custom.

We reached the bus stop accompanied by many villagers. A few of them came with us till Jaipur. When the bus moved out of Khedli, we waved to the villagers. Reaching Jaipur I fell sick. Our friends from Khedli decided to stay till my recovery. They sobbed and wept when we finally bid goodbye and proceeded from Jaipur to Ahmedabad.

CHAPTER NINE

BEHIND THE VEIL . . .

by

KUMKUM RAI

Kumkum Rai has M.A. in Anthropology from Lucknow University. Before joining this project, she worked in a project, organized by CARE. She along with her husband, joined Indian Institute of Management, Ahmedabad after completion of SITE.
Kumkum Rai was born and brought up in a Bengali/Hindi speaking family in Uttar Pradesh. She was educated in Lucknow, the medium of instruction being Hindi and English.

Departing the village

BEHIND THE VEIL . . .

—KUMKUM RAI

ABOUT THE VILLAGE

THE STATE of Rajasthan is divided into twentysix districts. Sawai Madhopur is one of the districts situated on the eastern border of Rajasthan. The village Khedli is located in the western part of Sawai Modhopur district. Jaipur is 121 km from Khedli. It is not an isolated village as it is situated on the Jaipur-Gangapur road. The village is accessible throughout the year and every half an hour the bus passes through the village. Population of the revenue village of Khedli is 1357, according to 1971 census.

Entering the village

My husband and I reached Khedli* on 22, October 1975. We spent the preceding night in Gangapur, a town located 21 km, east of Khedli. We were informed by the watchman here, that we could proceed to travel the following morning at 8 a.m. and reach the village at 9.30 a.m. The next morning, we started for Khedli, leaving our luggage behind. The bus would its way through the Tahsil headquarters, which was 6 km perpendicular to the main road and hence had to travel an extra 12 km on semi pucca road. We reached Khedli at about-10 a.m.

The first person whom I met in the village was the village school teacher, introduced by my husband. (my husband met the other primary school teachers). He then enquired if he could meet Suresh whom he had met in his earlier visit in October. Suresh, (aged around 20 years) and Swaroop were

*See footnote on page 97

acquaintances of my husband on whose assistance we relied for finding accommodation. Suresh however was not in the village on that day. Instead, his uncle, (father's younger brother) promised to give us a room in his house.

The room was small. But left with no other alternative, we accepted it. We went back to the school. The school teacher enquired about the rent, and when we mentioned the rent to be Rs. 25, he declared, "the rent is too much... I will call Swaroop and will make better arrangements."

While discussing about the rent, Munni a young girl, aged around ten years walked up to me and smiling, invited me to her home. I accompanied her to her home where I met her mother and her sister-in-law. The first question I was asked was "What is your jati ? What is your *Gotra* ?" to which I replied that I was a Brahmin and my Gotra was Bhardwaj. This of course was a lie. However, they were pleased. They were also happy to learn that we were staying in the village for one year. Munni's mother stated that they belonged to the Brahmin jati and that there were very few Brahmin households in Khedli.

Kameri, a girl of Munni's age was present during the interchange of words. She requested me to visit her home as well. I welcomed her invitation, for I was keen on building a rapport with the villagers. Kameri was also a Brahmin living with her widowed mother and uncle (father's younger brother). I stayed with them till noon. At half past one, my husband asked me to accompany him to see the new house arranged by Swaroop. I visited the premises. The house had two small rooms with a verandah in front. I liked it. The pucca double storyed building was situated in the central market place. This building belonged to Dayal Kandelwal. Three shops opening to three verandahs was on the ground floor. These shops were owned by the three Dayal brothers. The first floor had three rooms and a verandah. We occupied two of the rooms while Avtar, the younger brother of Dayal lived with his family in the third. Dayal also owned another *kucha* house, where his family resided.

Dayal assured us that we could occupy the house the following day. He took me to his home and introduced me to Prem, wife of Chand his elder brother, Prem gave me a stool to sit. She was grinding gram, and all the while talking to me. A few minutes later, Angoori, Avtar's wife entered. I was introduced to her. She then joined Prem in the task of grinding gram. They asked me many questions. "Where is your mother's place ? What kind of class factions do you have in the city ?" They then enquired about my jati to confirm what Dayal had told them. They were happy to learn that we were to stay in Khedli for some time. I stayed at their home till 5.30 p.m. It had started drizzling by then and it was refreshing to sip a cup of tea while waiting to proceed to the school. At 5.30 p.m. I went to the school where the school teacher in formed me that the electricity had gone and hence the TV viewing in the evening was cancelled. I was advised to return to Gangapur. My husband and I boarded the bus leaving for Gangapur to 6.30 p.m.

Settling down in Khedli

The next morning at 10.30 a.m. my husband and I shifted our luggage to Khedli. Angoori and Prem assisted me in the task of arranging the house. Within two days, the news about our arrival had spread throughout the village. The villagers referred to my husband as *television-wala* (person associated with TV). Thus in the process of arranging the house, three to four women came to see me. One of them began talking to Prem, and then introduced me to the others. I was to find later, that these two women were money lenders. Women of the lower jatis who were poor could borrow a sum of around Rs. 10 to 20 from them. They were a good asset in providing links for friendships with women of the lower jati. Draupati, a Brahmin aged sixteen years and Rampati, a Gujjar aged twenty years also assisted me in building a rapport with the village women.

The village women curious by nature, asked me many questions at the first instance—my husband's salary, duration of our stay in the village and other personal details. I also secured the friendship of the village men which was accepted by the villagers since I was given the role of a married women. The villagers were very suspicious. They believe that my husband would take their photographs for telecasting. They believed that his task was to "open and close" the TV. Hence, when they observed him taking attendance of TV viewers and filling up the observation sheets, they were certain that he would send their names to the government to impose a tax of fifty rupees per person for TV viewing. A rumour spread to this effect. But of course, we convinced them of our best intentions and the rumour was curtailed.

I did not tell the village women about my profession and work. I merely convinced them that I was in Khedli since I wanted to be with my husband, and being educated I assisted him in his work. I followed the local custom of maintaining *purdah*. I created a good impression among the villagers and won their approval and friendship which served as an asset to my work.

Life in Khedli—events and issues

In the beginning of my stay, Angoori hardly visited her room during the day. Her husband visited her during the nights. But this pattern changed in the course of time, and I observed that she visited her room after work. Angoori introduced me to the women in the neighbourhood. Since my home was situated in a multi-jati locality, my interaction with the neighbours included women of various jatis.

Facing opposite my home was a double storeyed building owned by Swaroop, cousin of Dayal. On one side of this house were two Brahmin households and on the other a Nai (barber) household. A Brahmin family resided next to the Nai household and opposite to this was the residence of a Kumahar. In front of the Nai household, a Mahajan family resided in a pucca single storeyed house. Behind my house, were the houses of Lohar families. I soon became friendly with the women in my neighbourhood.

After two months, I left Khedli. I fell sick and hence returned to my home in Lucknow. In my absence, the village women helped my husband in household chores. They cooked his meals and cleaned and swept the rooms. I returned after twenty days. I was touched by their concern and affection to me. They enquired about my health and expressed their grief over my illness and absence. After this incident, we were always posed with the question "When will you return ?" before we set out on any official tour, and if we did not return on the expected date, they would voice their complaint.

The last days in Khedli

We received orders on 24, September 1976 asking us to wind

up our field work. This whole episode was so dramatic that when I recall it, it flashes in my mind with a tinge of nostalgia. Dinesh Khandelwal, delivered five letters, having collected it from the post office, three kilometres away at around 7 p.m. One of these letters was from the headquarters, asking us to reach Ahmedabad by 11, October 1976. We informed Dinesh about the contents of the letter to which he said "I am the unlucky fellow who brought these letters and now you have to leave Khedli." We consoled him—"The postman would have delivered the letter tomorrow if you had not brought them. So do not feel so upset. We would have had to leave sooner or later . . . ."

He left after a while and on his way home, informed Dayal, our house owner. Dayal came running, enquiring if the news conveyed to him was true. Soon, the news about our return to Ahmedabad spread througout the village. The villagers had not considered about our leaving Khedli seriously. They believed that they would make arrangements for our stay. The news of our departure spread like bush fire. The men who gathered in the market place for gossip sessions in the nights were the first to learn about our departure. They informed the women. The next day morning, the women exchanged the news while fetching water from the village wells.

Hence, within twenty four hours the news had reached one and all. The villagers visited us in turns, requesting us to stay for *Deepawali*, a festival due on 22nd October. We replied "We have to report on 11, October 1976, and hence we have to go on 6, October 1976." I was surprised to learn that the villagers were trying to stop our departure. They had, within a few days after hearing the news, jointly written a petition to send to our head office in Ahmedabad. I also learnt that the women were ready to pay a small amount for this cause. We had to convince them that it was not possible for us to stay back in Khedli. On hearing this, one of the villagers commented sarcastically. "They are just not interested in staying in Khedli."

With the closing approach of our departure we visited the villagers homes for meals. Everyday we were invited to different households for meals. So much so, that during the last three days, I did not have to cook my meals. The villagers sat with us the night preceding our departure. The women sat with me till 12.30 a.m. and the men till 4 a.m. conversing throughout the night. On the 6th morning, we had to have three breakfasts and four teas to appease the villagers. The women started weeping. At 8 a.m. the villagers made us sit on the verandah and placed a garland round our necks. The priest Krishna Sharma recited Sanskrit versus and placed *vermilion* on our foreheads. They then gave us Rs. 101. "It is our custom when our daughters join their husbands, we give this as our token of love . . . ." We accepted Rs. 11.

All the villagers were present during the farewell ceremony. We walked down to the road to catch the bus. Hundred women and girls stood with me waiting for the bus. While waiting for the bus a Gujjar women came to me with a glass of milk and said "I was making *rotis* for my husband. I came here to see you. I had not invited you to my home during your stay . . . so please drink this milk. It is the first and the last time." She said this with affection and warm that I could not refuse her. So, inspite of the heavy breakfast, I drank up the whole glass of milk.

The bus arrived at 9 a.m. The villagers compelled the drivers to retain the bus for half an hour. Two of my husband's friends came with us to Jaipur and eleven of them travelled with us till Lalsot (21 km). The villagers stood on the road waving with tears in their eyes and the bus moved out of the village.

CHAPTER TEN

THE 'GHOST' VILLAGE . . . .

K.K. PANDEY

K.K. Pandey, M.A. in Sociology from Patna University joined this project as a Research Fellow of A.N. Sinha Institute of Social Sciences. Later, he completed his Ph.D. using SITE data. He is presently a lecturer in Sociology in Bhagalpur University.

Pandey was born and brought up in Hindi speaking family of Bihar. He was educated in Bihar, Hindi/English being the medium of instruction in school and college.

With the informant

THE 'GHOST' VILLAGE . . . .

—K.K. PANDEY

ABOUT THE VILLAGE

BHUTERA is located in Gobindgarh block of Jaipur district, about 65 km southeast of Jaipur city. The nearest railway station is Chota Guda which is 6 km and the nearest village connected by bus is Hasteda, 4 km from Bhutera. Three rivers, Manda, Baroli and Alisar Wali join to form one river in the south and east of the village. The village has a middle school, an Ayurvedic dispensary and a branch post office. The headquarters of Patwari and the office of the Gram Panchayat are located in the village. The total population according to 1971 Census is 1353.

Entering the village

I left Jaipur in the morning of 21, March 1975.* Stopping at the Block Development Office, on the way to pick up the Block Development Officer, I reached Bhutera in the evening at 4 p.m. He introduced me to the Sarpanch and some villagers who were present. He asked the Sarpanch to take care of my accommodation and food. It was an order rather than a request. Or so his tone conveyed. After the exchange of greetings, I suggested

*K.K. Pandey had initial difficulties of staying in the village for eighteen months. Just after a few weeks of field work, he suffered from allergy which forced him to make constant visits to Jaipur, several times. Even while he was in the village, he was incapacitated to do field work for several weeks. At a later stage, due to personal problems he had a difficult time in the village. Some of these difficulties are reflected in his description. In spite of physical and personal problems and difficulty in communication, he completed his field work and was able to participate in all the workshops and meetings, alongwith the other anthropologists.

that we take a walk around the village. While conversing, a young man, probably aged around 25 years came forward, shook hands and introduced himself "I am Raju".

He accompanied me. We walked around the circular road around the Garh, while Raju pointed out the different settlements Brahmins, Kumhawats, Meena and Nai. I did not meet many villagers. Raju continued to speak, all the time boasting about himself or his influence in the village. I realised that Raju would be of assistance. When I returned from the walk, the Block Development Officer expressed his desire to leave. The driver was also restless since he wanted to be on the road before dusk. I bade them goodbye. The Sarpanch (headman) accompanied the Block Development Officer.

I was worried about finding accommodation, and thinking about it to myself, I turned to Raju and suggested that we have a cup of tea. Raju took me to a tea stall. A group of villagers were seated in a circle, talking in their local dialect, Dhundhari. Raju told me that they were talking about me. I greeted them with the customary *Ram Ram*. They in turn greeted me in a full throated chorus. I was given a bench to sit, facing them.

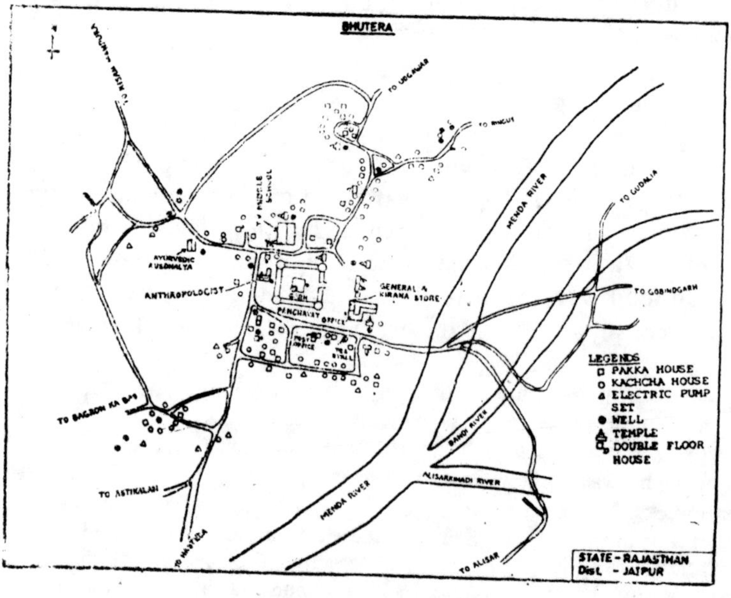

Village map of Bhutera

Raju introduced me "This is Pandey, from Bihar. He belongs to the Brahmin jati". He also introduced the villagers one by one. After the formal introduction, I told them the purpose of my visit to the village and my affiliation with the A.N. Sinha Institute of Social Studies and Space Applications Centre. I also explained that I would be staying in the village for more than a year, to complete the research study.

In the course of the conversation, I raised the issue of accommodation and food. Surajmal Sharma, a Brahmin working for a cloth merchant in Jamshedpur, Bihar, offered me a room and suggested that I dine with his family. I accepted the invitation. I stayed with him for a week. The week however was torturous, for the food offered to me consisting of thick barleygram—wheat, mixed bread, curry made of gram flour, turmeric powder, ghee and chilly was hot and spicy. I could not eat more that a morsel. It was a week of starvation and I survived on the few packets of biscuits that I had brought from Jaipur.

My home in Bhutera

I finally found a decent place to reside. It was a room in the first floor of a house, situated in the middle of the village. The room had a wide opening to the roof of the building from where I could get a clear view of the central village. The installation of TV was here. Within a week, I had established a good rapport with the villagers. Raju was very helpful. He managed to get a spring cot, a stool, a stove and a few cooking utensils. The stove and the utensils were his own. I now began cooking my meals. I had to fetch water for drinking and washing from a distance. Raju however helped me. Within a few weeks, I had to leave for Jaipur. Skin eruptions due to allergy appeared on my right hand finger and hence I had to leave to Jaipur for treatment.* I returned to Bhutera after a month.

Interaction with villagers

In the beginning the villagers were sceptical about my role.

*Due to some allergy or unknown cause, Pandey's right hand finger swelled and the skin errupted which kept him out of field work. It was very difficult for him to work.

When I went to meet a farmer in his farm, he would either shut off the pump or leave his farm. He would refuse to speak to me. This, Raju explained was due to their suspicion and fear that I was a government official. Government officials from the Revenue, Electricity and Police Department often harassed the villagers and fleeced them either directly or when afforded by an opportunity. My attempt to convince them about my academic research work would have failed, but for Raju's co-operation.

Raju made an attempt to convince them that I would be writing and publishing a book about them and their village, and hence the more open they were about their problems and issues, the more chances for solutions, since they would be notified to the government. Raju was, at times dramatic. He exaggerated and made false promises to them that I would note down all the problems faced by the common villagers. The villagers asked "But why only Bhutera ?" to which Raju replied "Because, Bhutera is one of the most underdeveloped villages of Rajasthan, and hence afforded a representative sample of the problem of the common villager".

I began the census survey which involved a door to door visit. Raju accompanied me in my field work. He was an interpreter between the villagers and me, since the villagers could not comprehend Hindi and I did not know their local dialect. I was dependent on Raju completely, and this was frustrating. I realised that I would have to learn the local dialect as well to win the confidence of some informants.

Soon, I began to settle down. In the course of time, I could understand Dhundhari, though I could not speek. The location of my room was also useful in providing an opportunity for interaction with the villagers. Situated in the centre of the village, with a wide roof, there was enough room to accommodate many villagers. The *Jat Patels* (jati headmen), elder Brahmins, Kumhawats and Meena often visited me in my room, perhaps to ascertain that I was a trustworthy person. Their reason for visiting me, they stated, was to be in the company of an educated person which they enjoyed.

On the groundfloor of the house was a *chakki*, operated in the evenings. Hence, some of them could have, on the pretext of grinding flour, spent time with me and referred to it as "passing-time-meanwhile." However my friendly approach and my willingness to greet and welcome everyone, soon won the confidence of the village headmen and elders. They began talking to me in a friendly manner.

During mid-July 1975, the *Naib Tahsildar*, a revenue official had come on a "hurricane tour" to the villages of Gobindgarh Block. He was on a mission to collect wheat levy from the farmers who had defaulted. During my afternoon walk through the village, I passed through the market place to find four farmers bowed and buckled in the posture of a hen as a punishment. A few policemen and a plain clothsman were kicking them with their boots. I did not understand what it was all about.

I walked upto the plain-clothsman, enquired his name and department he belonged to. I then requested him to come to accompany me to my room. He did so. The Naib Tahsildar argued that the farmers had defaulted and hence should be given such punishments. I declared that in a democracy, such things cannot be so. Morever, I pointed out, "Your job is the collection of levy. But the citizen has a right to live with dignity and he cannot be denied of this." "Neither do you have magisterial power to give such punishment. You cannot take the law into your hands." He agreed. After a cup of tea, he departed.

This incident had a profound effect in gaining the confidence of the villagers. After this, I found it easy to mingle among the villagers as a friend. I even came to be accepted as a family member in a number of Brahmin, Mahajan, Jat, Rajput and Kumhawat households.

Informants

Jugal Kishore Rawat, the lone-Kirana shop owner and D.S. Dixit, a school teacher in the local middle school were two of my close confidants. Jugal, aged 22, had completed his high school. He supplied me with the daily provisions. He became a good friend. During my interaction, he was convinced that I was a researcher and that I would not harm the villagers. Jugal was a wealthy trader, owning the local Kirana shop. His shop was a meeting place for many villagers and hence he was successful in his attempt to convince them about my good intentions.

CHAPTER ELEVEN

INSTRUCTIONS FOR FIELD WORK

by

—BINOD C. AGRAWAL
—J.K. DOSHI
—K.K. VARMA

These instructions were prepared over a long period of time by the Project Leaders and were sent to all the anthropologists in the field. These instructions were also discussed among the anthropologists when they visited Ahmedabad.

J.K. Doshi Ph.D in Anthropology from Saugar University worked as co-Project Leader of this study. Currently, he is Professor, Department of Agriculture Communication G.B. Pant University of Agriculture and Technology. Doshi was born and brought up in a Hindi speaking family from Rajasthan. He was educated in Rajasthan and Madhya Pradesh, Hindi/English being the medium of instruction in school and college.

K.K. Verma, Ph.D in Anthropology from Ranchi University, prior to joining this project was a fellow of A.N. Sinha Institute of Social Studies, Patna. Currently he is an Associate Professor and Head at Rajendra Agricultural University, PUSA.
Verma was born in a Hindi speaking family of Bihar. He was educated in Hindi and English, being the medium of instruction in school and college.

APPENDICES

APPENDIX—I

VILLAGE SOCIAL RESEARCH HOUSEHOLD CENSUS 1975

1	2	3	4	5	6	7

FORM : *REC*/050

Serial No.

8-11. House Number (if any please write) :
What is your name ?
12. What is the name of your Muhalla/Para :
13. Since how long have you been living in the village with your family ?
14. Who has the responsibility of your household ?
15. Does he look after every work of the household ?
16. What is the total number of persons who eat and live together in this household ? (Write the actual number)
17. Please trace the household genealogy :
(Age, Education and Name)

Kindly circle the household members

Fill the data after completion of the work only

Sr. No.	Name	Relation-ship to ego	Sex	Age	Edu-cation	Occu-pation

18. What is your religion ?
    1. Hindu
    2. Muslim
    3. Sikh
    4. Christian
    5. Jain
    6. Buddhist
    7. Specify if any other
19. What is your jati ?
20. What kind of............are you and what is your Gotra or its equivalent ?
    (Before asking add the answer of question 19 in blank space, please probe)
21. What are the jatis with whom you have food exchange relationship ?
22. What are the jati/jatis with whom you have marriage relationship ?

23. Do you have any first degree relative/relatives (by blood or by marriage) in this village....No/Yes, if yes, please give their names and addresses.
24. What is your family occupation (kindly list all the occupations given by the respondents)
25. (If agriculture in question 23) kindly ask about the total land cultivated by the household members.
26. What was your forefather's occupation ?
27. What language do you speak in the house ?
28. What language/languages do you speak while in market/ business or away from the village ?
29. Are there any person/persons in your household who can speak languages other than mentioned in 26, and 27 ?
30. Observe the house type (Kachha, Pucca, mixed asbestos-sheet/tin/hut etc.) PLEASE PROBE FOR CLARIFICATION.
31. Is there any radio/transistor in your household ?
    No/Yes, If yes, what kind and how many ?
32. Do you/any member of your household receive any newspaper/weekly, etc. ?
    No/Yes. If yes, give detail.
33. Dose any member of your household go to see movies ?
    No/Yes, If yes, give detail.

HOLISTIC STUDY

FORM : REC : 051 *For internal use only*

INSTRUCTIONS FOR HOUSEHOLD CENSUS DATA COLLECTION

The aim of village census is three-fold (a) to collect accurate demographic data of the village, (b) to familiarize the anthropologist with the village people, and, (c) to build rapport in the village.

In terms of accuracy of the data the most important aspect is the census. It is important to note that anthropological census taking differs from the normal census as our interest is much wider.

1. Kindly use one village Social Research "Household Census 1975" Schedule for each house-hold. The household is defined as persons living and eating together and may or may not be relatives. For example, in this way a servant is a member of the household in case he/she stays in the same house and eats.

2. While asking questions please use local dialect. The schedule is a guide for you. But remember that the questions must be asked using anthropological research tools.

3. Please write as many details as possible. Even if the question happened to be close ended, you must write all details if you think it is important to note. *Remember you are not filling a questionnaire.* Use the left hand side of the Schedule which is left blank for this purpose.

ON THE SCHEDULE

8—11. This question has been asked for household identification.

12. This question has been asked to identify the residential identification related to areas where the person is living. In future it will allow us to understand how the spatial sub-division of a village is associated with the name of a particular jati, religious group, etc.

13. This question has been asked to know the length of inter-personal relationships with other villagers. Check in detail if they are migrants, the reasons of migration etc.

14—15. These questions have been asked to know the name of the head of household as perceived by the respondents.

16. This question has been asked to know the household size. Make sure that respondent does not include those persons who are not living in the household at that time for an extended period.

17. Trace the household genealogy. Please see that all the members living or dead or migrated should be incorporated in genealogical table using usual anthropological symbols. Each member should be described by socio-cultural characteristic in data pool which include name, age, sex, education, occupation, important information, etc. Servant or other distant related persons should be mentioned in the note of that household.

18. This question is asked to know the religion. Please circle the one who belongs to particular religion.

19. This question is asked in the broadest sense. You must record whatever the respondent says.

20. Write the gotra of a Hindu only. For non-Hindus write further details.

21. This question has been asked to know the extent to which the individual can interact within the village situation. In addition this will allow to delimit the social boundaries of the jati.

22. This question is final test of the jati boundary. Please ask this question very carefully.

23. This question will be helpful to the network and social extension of the respondent. Later this question will be needed to isolate various "social groups" for studying communication pattern.

24. This question has been asked to know the occupation of the household.

25. This question is related to the earlier question no. 24. In case the respondent belongs to a agricultural house this question should be asked. DO NOT CONVERT

LOCAL BIGHA/measurement to standard measurement. We will do later.

26. This question has been asked to know the "traditional occupation".
27. This question has been asked to know the language spoken within the walls of household. We will use this question later to evaluate the impact of television on speech and spoken language.
28. This question has been asked to measure the bilingulism.
29. This question has been asked for the same reason as those question no. 28.
30. This question has been asked to measure the economic status of the household. Please observe carefully before writing in detail.

31—33. These three questions are asked to know the level of communication expose, if any, in the household.

From questions 19-22 are used for Isolating Jati of the respondent.

FORM REC/052

WHEN SITE ANTHROPOLOGIST IS AT WORK

Remember you are a 'native' anthropologist and studying your own people. Your whole approach towards field work must be different then those of foreign anthropologists Most of the books, on field methods are written from the 'foreign's' point of view for the study of the 'native'. Our effort will be to develop a new methodology for the study of our own people. As a member of the larger linguistic region you share most of the broad values and beliefs of your people. The most important of all is that you speak the same language as your informants speak. In other words, you do not have to spend any time in learning the language. But you will have to adopt the local dialect and style of speech. Your individual social background in most cases will determine your status in the village. Be 'objective' on this point. Accept it as a 'fact'. In due course of time, your own relationships with various individuals in the village will change your status. By that time you will be in a most comfortable position. Modesty and honesty pays.

BE AWARE

Being a native anthropologist your quality of field work may be questioned as you can not be very 'objective' The main argument against your field work will be that your personal bias would influence your observations. Argue back—the advantage of language and effect of good training would minimize any bias. After all anthropological field work is individualized personal experience. Make sure to maintain an independent and neutral position in the village. On many occasions you will have to take sides. Watch out. Do not take sides as far as possible. Try to locate your 'pole of observation' in a centrally located place,

Do not expect any special treatment of any kind from your village people. It leads to all kinds of status confusions and complications.

In financial terms, spend no more than the amount a university Junior Research Fellow can afford to spend during your field work.

GUIDE FOR WRITING FIELD NOTES AND DIARIES

The field diary of an anthropologist is the basic document which contains *all the data* collected by him/her. It must be preserved *very carefully* and should be kept *confidential*.

Precision and micro-detailed descriptions are the essence of anthropological field work. YOU MUST WRITE ALL OBSERVATIONS IN DETAIL. WRITE FACTS AND INTERPRETATIONS SEPARATELY. Conversations should be written as far as possible in the language of the informants. Verbal details are most desirable. There are two kinds of field notes: (a) taking notes on the spot; (b) writing detailed daily diary. Majority of the field data are collected while talking or observing some festival, ceremonies etc. It is extremely difficult to take down notes on the spot. In few cases like in 'funeral' one cannot take notes on the spot. In such a situation you should not try to take field notes. Rather you should make, if extremely necessary, few small notes in pocket diary, which you must carry on every occasion.

Daily field diary

You must write every day your 'daily field diary'. Here you must write in detail (a) field notes on your observations, (b) field notes on your discussion, conversations (c) details about interpersonal communication, gossips, the folk history and other similar events, and (d) specific details of some special event like 'marriage and festival'.

Special reference must be made about the main area of your study. For example, the details about the process of message diffusion, various kinds of channels of communication must be described in detail.

It is extremely important to distinguish clearly between

observation and *interpretation*. In your field diary, theory and fact should not be merged. Yoy may construct a 'theoretical model' that you would like to test. Please write this separately and only after recording the 'facts'.

Language of your field notes

In the process of translation from one language to another one looses the meaning, expression etc. Secondly the linguistic ability of an individual anthropologist also influences the translation. It is recommended that you should try to write your field notes in local language as far as possible. You must write all specific terms in the local language like kinship terms. It will help you in getting good quality data. Later at the time of report writing we will together translate the field diary into English.

Setting up

The first question you will encounter even before you can take up your residence in the village is 'who are you?' and 'what is the purpose of your stay in the village?' Please be very clear about these two points. Your answer will be that you want to study the impact of TV on the village life and you belong to Research and Evaluation Cell of Space Applications Centre, Ahmedabad. In case of Research Fellows of A.N. Sinha Institute, they will associate themselves with A.N. Sinha Institute, Patna. Please repeat the same statement no matter how many times you are asked this question. Do not feel irritated to repeat. For heavens sake *do not* change your statement. You will be asked about your salary : tell the truth about the basic salary.

In the village, try not to take too many obligations. Remember that every obligation must be reciprocated. Set up your household independently. It is extremely and essential for your field work. By maintaining a separate household you will be able to maintain your independent position in the village which will help in your field work.

Your camera

It is expected that you will have only one Yashica square size camera, in which you can use 120 and 35 mm films. Try to use 120 films. Use your camera carefully and keep it will utmost care. Films will be supplied to you. Keep your films in cool place. In case you need more films request Associate Scientist or buy when you are in the city.

Use of camera

Camera is an essential element in the anthropologist's kit for field work. It allows you to record events like rituals, festivals, marriages, death etc. In addition, it gives a chance to catch visually the life style of the people. But you are fully aware that you cannot photograph many events in your village due to local aversion towards photography. For example, taking photographs of the temple deities and many ceremonial occasions are not allowed. It is strongly suggested to use your camera only in that situation where you are allowed to do so.

Another problem you may face is that people will demand copies of their photographs. Please do not make false promises. It is easy to say but difficult to keep with it. But you must have to cultivate the habit of saying politely 'No'. In case you promise to give photographs you have to pay from your own pocket. Do not blame the organization later. Another problem you will face is that people in the village will invite you to take photographs and will promise to pay for film and processing. It is advisable to avoid but if you have to do the job, do it without expecting any payment.

Processing of the films

Please mark every film role. Send it to cluster headquarters or bring it to cluster headquarters where generally you should get it processed. Keep your negatives in negative files properly indexed. Write details of the negative content. It will help you while writing report. In case you shoot some colour transparancies get it processed through Associate Scientist. Please take as many photographs as possible. Be clear in your mind why you want to take a particular photograph. This will help you later in writing and also using these photographs instead of one. Action pictures are best. Try as far as possible to take photographs in natural and action situation.

Your tape recorder

Tape recorder is a tool for data collection. It can only be

used in interviews and for recording a song or music or dialogue. It can also be used where you want verbatim data. Tape recorder in this respect is a handy tool to have for more accurate data. But it has certain inherent limitations :

1. Informants generally become very conscious of tape recorder and the nature of conversation changes. Many a times they feel very suspicious and refuse to talk. On the other occasions, they like to hear what they have said. In each case use of tape recorder becomes a hinderance in field work.
2. Keeping the proper indexing of the tapes are another problem.
3. Many a time after recording is done you may forget to write other details which may effect later analysis.

Use of tape recorder

1. Use your tape recorder only after developing a good rapport in the village.
2. Before starting any recording please make sure to give data place of interview, subject/topic of discussion tape number, if any. After the completion of the interview you must repeat the same exercise.
3. On the top of the Cassette space is provided for identification purposes. Please do use the space for this purpose.
4. A separate operation manual will be provided to you, please read it carefully before using the tape recorder.

All used cassettes should be kept in cool and safe place.

PRE-SITE FIELD WORK

The first few weeks of residence in the village involve a plan of work which will allow you to observe the physical and social arrangement of the village. This you can do by mapping the village, making a household census, use census schedule No Form REC/050 supplied separately. Genealogies provide the necessary information regarding various relations of the various households which will be useful in tracing out the social contacts of the villagers. A map has to be drawn in such a way that is shows the physical features like streams, springs, streets, hills, rivers, temples, ponds, fields etc. It is also helpful in identifying the property, neighbourhoods, direction of village growth, and will be useful while taking census.

It is also important to note down all the available information regarding various diseases, general celebration, for meeting these diseases and the deities connected with diseases. This information has to be annexed by the information collected from the health centres available in the vicinity of your village.

DURING SITE

By the time SITE starts and the programmes come over the TV the anthropologist will be able to locate the key informants and the leaders in the village. The maintenance of relations, especially with key informants demands that the anthropologists maintain a discrete silence about every interview and observational data and try not to be drawn into personal disputes of any kind. It is also *unwise* and *unethical* to try to trade off the information gained from one informant in hope of getting more information from another person.

During SITE you can play the role of participant observer to the maximum extent possible. SITE envisages broadcast of two sets of programmes, morning programmes for the school going children in the age groups of 5-11 and the evening for the adults relating to various rural developmental programmes. You must observe the reactions to the programmes and their participation in the viewing of the programmes accordingly.

You must set your timings depending on the broadcast timings. It is necessary for you to contact the villagers in the morning to discuss the overnights programme before they make a start to their fields. Generally the villagers leave their houses very early. Please set your interview timings according to the convenience of the villagers. Villagers may not be in a mood to discuss in the night after the completion of viewing as they get tired after a strenous day and will be in a mood to sleep. Hence it is better to contact them in the morning. About children's programme you can participate in their activity and can discuss and elicit the answers by taking to them by acting as one of them. All this can be done by 12 noon. It is advisable to go to the fields where the villagers are engaged in working for observing the adaption process. You may also discuss during their work about the things they have seen during the night. This necessitates you to spend your entire day along with the villagers either they are children or adults. The adults can also be invited to discussion while they take rest around 6 O' clock in the evening on their pials after coming from the work prior to taking their dinner.

The information diffusion to neighbouring villages can be recorded by making visits to the neighbouring villages as and when you find time. For this purpose you must keep record of visitors for viewing TV in the village. You must identify them and contact them in their villages. This will allow you to understand inter-village channels of communications.

POST SITE FIELD WORK

By the end of SITE you will become aware not only of various communication channels, but also of the adaption and diffusion processes, impact of TV programmes in various spheres of village life.

Post SITE village study aims at finding out the impact of TV programmes and how long this impact lasts in the village. There may be a gap of two to three months after the during SITE study and post SITE study. During this period the anthropologists will be writing reports based on the information collected in the field work. After the report writing is complete anthropologists return to the field. In this period you must observe the impact left by SITE on the villagers. How far the information has diffused. How deep the SITE information has penetrated into the daily life of the villagers? How the SITE has affected the cultural patterns of villagers?

Termination of field work

Although everybody knows in the beginning that the researcher's stay in the village is a temporary one, an atmosphere of permanancy almost and always evolves and develops among the villagers, with the contracts developed by the anthropologist.

In our rural conditions where a number of government

officials are transferred on regular basis your termination will be treated in the same way. Although your informants and other will feel sad, please try to be as calm as possible on this occasion. You may consider to dispose off few of your belongings. It is suggested that you should try to bring it out as it may create some confusion as to whom you give what ?

APPENDIX-III

FORM : REC/054

BROAD AREAS OF DATA COLLECTION

Demographic Situation

Density of population—No. of males and females (Census) yearly birth and death rates. (See also under household). Migration—Seasonal/permanent—with specific emphasis on 'push' and 'pull' factors.

Geographical situation

Climate—rainfall—land—rivers—forest—hills—terrain—tanks—ponds—drainage. (Secondary data will be collected from District Gazetteers/Census Handbook, Land Revenue Record and other official documents).

Social Ecology (Tolas/Dhani etc.)

Villagers concept of village boundary—boundary of the revenue village—boundary made by the people of the village—i.e. different levels of interaction. Spatial network.

Economic situation

Sources of livelihood—agriculture, carpentary, blacksmithy, shopkeeping, basketarry, pottery, labour, industries, animal husbandry, fishing, service of the priest, service and others.

Agriculture—land—type—nature of the soil—fertility of the soil—irrigated—unirrigated —land— tenure—their terms and conditions. Crops : Rabi and Kharif—crop cycle and crop rotation—improved seed. Extent of availability—agricultural practices—traditional : ploughing, digging, levelling etc. Modern tractors, power tilling etc. Agricultural Implements—Modern (new) Traditional (old). Methods of irrigation—means of irrigation—Crops diseases—measures of controlling pests—traditional and modern. Uses of manures—chemical fertilizers—extent of availability and sources—agencies operting in the area such as Block-Co-operatives for the agricultural development.

Identify the various agencies operating in the village. Industries—small scale—large scale. Labourers—types—agricultural—industrial wage system—terms and conditions.

Extent of indebtedness—sources—terms and conditions. Marketing of the produce—means of transportation of the produces—upto the market—village—market—weekly, bi-weekly etc. Nearest town and its influence on village.

Political organization

Leadershipstructure—formal—informal. Political institutions—village, panchayat—caste panchayat etc. participation in various political/semi political institutions.

Social organization

Marriage forms, monogamous, polygamous, terms and conditions for marriage—ceremonies—age of marriage—widow marriage—views of the community about widow—marriage—divorce—opinion of the villagers about it. Remarriage and divorces—of male—of female. Attitudes about intercaste marriage. Household types, attitude towards family planning, practice of family planning.

Family—size and composition—family types in the village. Intra family relationships—husband—wife—parents—child—mother-in-law—daughter-in-law—joking, relationship—avoidance relationship.

Religious organisation—village priest—religious practices. Magico—religious beliefs associated with village deities. Witchcraft and sorcery—activities of a sorcerer—cases of witchraft. Religious dogmas. Extent of dependence for cure of diseases on deities/witchcraft etc. Type of diseases treated by witchcraft. Participation in each other religious, function—respect/disrespect about other's religion—religious conflict if any. Social distance—social disabilities.

Folklore tradition and language—song, dance, story, legend, ballad, riddle, myth etc.—language spoken in the village.

Material culture

House pattern—dress pattern—food pattern and drinking habit—utensils—ornaments—implements.

Ventilation and sanitation consciousness, drainage, disposal of garbage, habits of natural call answering.

Games and amusements
Game types—castes of the children participating in the games.

Household data
Census data—age—sex—number of members in a household.

Genealogy
Number of members in a household—age—sex—occupation—primary—secondary—education—literate—illiterate.

Mapping
Map of the revenue village—map of the people's village boundary—Map of the households arrangement. Map of the agriculture—Irrigated unirrigated—cultivated—uncultivated lands.

APPENDIX-IV

FORM : *REC/56*

NOTE FOR THE ANTHROPOLOGIST IN THE FIELD

This note has been prepared keeping in mind that SITE is to commence 15 days from now. Therefore, it is essential that you must observe very carefully the details of what is happening in the village during this period. It will be advisable that you should observe the micro details of what kind of discussions are taking place regarding television. More specifically you should write detailed observations relating to the following questions. :

1. In which group of village television is a focal point of discussion ? Describe the group like youth educated etc. Describe the group where nothing is being discussed about TV, e.g. women, Harijans or other poor people may never discuss about TV in village.
2. What kind of rumours are being spread in the village regarding the appearance of TV in village ?
3. What kind of discussions are taking place regarding the reliable functioning of the TV ?
4. What is their notion about our technicians and their fixing of the TV ? Write in detail.
5. Are villagers planning to have any ceremony on inaugural day ? Write in detail if it is planned so.
6. Are there some individuals who are taking special interest in TV and its inaugural?
7. Observe if you think some conflicts would arise, like one group wanting to control the TV compared to other group.
8. Before SITE starts you must observe if relatives are invited, including daughters from nearby villages for the occasion.
9. Whether any one in the village is planning to have any ritual performance on this day ?
10. The most important point for observation is to describe in detail the expectation of village people of TV, e.g. do

they expect that they will be able to get more entertainment from TV? Do they believe that TV would spoil the youth of the village ?

11. In general we also must try to measure the varying opinions of various age groups, jati groups and males and females.
12. As far as possible you must intermingle with kids between the age groups of 5 to 12 and ask their opinion about TV, expectations and beliefs about TV. At this occasion it may be good that you quietly follow children in their games or walks and try to note down their discussions.

August 1, 1975

On this day we expect to have inauguration of our television programmes. There will be no programmes in the morning. Therefore, you can not observe children. In the evening, at 6.20 p.m. the actual inauguration will take place. After 10 minutes of inauguration message (it is expected that Prime Minister will give speech, but yet not fully decided) the actual programme will start. The programme schedule will follow the following sequence :

1. August 1, 1975—October 31, 1975
2. April 1, 1976—July 31, 1976

6.20 p.m.—7.00 p.m. Andhra & Karnataka
7.00 p.m.—7.30 p.m. Common (News & Integration)
7.30 p.m.—8.10 p.m. Orissa & Madhya Pradesh
8.10 p.m.—8.50 p.m. Bihar & Rajasthan

November 1, 1975—March 31, 1976

6.00 p.m.—6.40 p.m. Bihar & Rajasthan
6.40 p.m.—7.10 p.m. Common (News & Integration)
7.10 p.m.—7.50 p.m. Orissa & Madhya Pradesh
7.50 p.m.—8.30 p.m. Andhra Pradesh & Karnataka

Your first job today will be to observe at what time people started gathering near TV. You must assess the audience in the following categories :

(1) Villagers, (2) Villagers' relatives and friends who are there as invitee and outsiders (those who are coming from other villages and not invited), (3) Male and female, various age groups, religious groups like Hindu, Muslims, Christians, etc. Within Hindu various jati groups. Please try to observe

the sitting pattern and the spatial positions with respect to TV taken by various jati groups, religious groups, male and female. It may be a good idea to draw a map and indicate the locations of various individuals. Try to reach the TV place about an hour or two hours earlier and stay there even when the programmes are over.

During the programme, try to observe and listen to the discussion of the viewers and their reactions. Try to talk to some informant and write down their reactions about TV programme.

Objectively try to evaluate the quality of picture e.g. picture might become blurred, hazy, nonvisible, etc. You must write these details. Observe if people stay and talk about the programme after it is over.

Observe if any rituals were performed this day. If sweets were distributed, if some big man, officials are invited on this occasion you must write all this in detail,

It will be advisable that during this period you should speak little and listen more. Straight questions should be asked instead of loaded ones like "What is your opinion about programme". The answer may be noted without providing any suggestion. There is a tendency to ask questions like "I am sure you must have liked the programme." Please DO NOT ask such questions.

Above all, you must write in detail the excitement and reaction of the people. If possible, you also note down each piece of information which you think was important and try to keep in your diary on the following day. Try to trace if the message was :

1. Reinterpreted for someone by a viewer.
2. How far the message has reached.
3. What was the level of distortion in the message. The term distortion here means simply how the message has been slanted and changed from the original to create desirable impact.
4. Whether these messages were discussed for clarification?

August 2

In the morning today the first programme for children will be beamed. You have to go to school, repeat the same observations as you have done in the previous evening for adults. The only additional information you need is about the teachers, their reactions towards TV and the students. In addition you should also observe how children react towards TV and how they talk among themselves. Do they look happy, bewildered, surprised, scared ?

Regular routine

Your day's schedule should be divided into four parts :

(1) Observing children in school as much as possible, (2) Evening audience observation and participation in TV viewing. (3) Collecting data on channels of communication and processes of change that are occurring in the village and (4) collecting data on various village institutions.

In addition you must collect data on special occasions, visits of outsiders, visits of various government officials, etc. Also the various channels of communications bringing new messages in village. In your diary all these information should be in detail and in duplicate.

DAILY TV VIEWING OBSERVATIONS SHEET

NAME OF CLUSTER ________ DISTRICT ________ VILLAGE ________ DATE ________

	1	2	3	4	5	6	7	8	9	10	11	12	13	14	15	16	17	18	19	20	21	22	23	24	25	26	27	28	29	30	31	32	33	34	35	36	37	38	39	40
1																																								
2																																								
3																																								
4																																								
5																																								
6																																								
7																																								
8																																								
9																																								
10																																								
11																																								
12																																								
13																																								
14																																								
15																																								
16																																								
17																																								
18																																								
19																																								
20																																								
21																																								
22																																								
23																																								
24																																								
25																																								

APPENDIX-V

FORM REC/055

TV VIEWING, PARTICIPATION, AUDIENCE AND THEIR REACTIONS

In the village from the first to the last day, audience will come to view TV programmes. A TV Quarterly diary is being maintained in the village by custodian. The data collected by him will provide information regarding the total viewers, their composition. What we would like to do is to measure and get actual data on (a) the viewers characteristics (b) viewers participation in discussion after TV programme viewing and (c) nature of their participation in other TV related activities.

A. In operational terms, we would like to maintain a daily 'Attendance diary'. One for children programme in the morning and other for adult programme in the evening. In these diaries we must keep the name of the viewer, age, sex, jati, religion, occupation and his/her sitting location. These observations should be made at least once in a week. In the register separate columns should be kept for outsiders, visitors and guests.

B. In the *Feedback study* a separate instrument has been prepared. It will not be desirable to collect data on feedback study every day. But you will have to interview audience on sample basis twice a month on selected days and programmes. The method followed in interviewing and selection of the audience will be as follows :

1. 1. From your adult 'Attendance Diary' you separate the adult population of both sexes. You take 15 respondents from your register at random. Interview them on the spot or next day, or on the same day depending upon the situation. The schedule filled by you should be sent to Ahmedabad within a week. This exercise will be repeated twice in a month.

1. 2. From your Children 'Attendance Diary' you should select 15 respondents twice a month on similar basis and

should interview 15 children. The schedule filled by you should reach Ahmedabad within a week.

It may happen that on a particular day the TV was not working while you were ready for interviewing. In that case, in your register you write that the TV was put off for the reasons—death, marriage of a villager and must mention that the TV was not functioning. Even in this case you must observe if some of the audience still visit the site for TV viewing. Take their attendance and ask why they had come to view TV.

Summary :

1. Fill 'Attendance Diary' once a week.
   (a) For children's programme (morning)
   (b) For adult programme (evening)
   (c) For adult National programme (in Hindi) for non-Hindi clusters (Gujarat, Andhra Pradesh & Karnataka).
2. Audience "Feedback Study" twice a month on 15 respondents each time among adults and among children.
3. Please do not forget to write in your daily diary about your own observations. REMEBER YOU MUST DESCRIBE PROCESS.

APPENDIX-VI

FORM : REC/057

A NOTE ON HOW TO COLLECT DATA ON QUALITATIVE FEED-BACK FROM 16TH DECEMBER TO 31ST DECEMBER 1975

Through the present system of our feed-back we are getting a statistical picture of what happens to the programmes that are broadcast for the audiences in various SITE clusters and Kheda district. While the quantitative information has its merit we sometimes like to get descriptive data also. Let us say, if the quantitative data forms the skeleton, the qualitative description provides flesh to the skeleton. Both are equally important.

Basically we are interested in knowing the following :

(1) How many people view TV programmes on the day of observation?

(2) What kind of interest is aroused by different programmes on a day ?

(3) How much of what we try to convey is (refer to specific programme) understood and whether the lack of comprehension (understanding) is due to difficulty of language, unfamiliar objects, bad presentation or any other reasons. Whether the theme is comprehended fully, partially or not at all ?

(4) What programmes are liked most and what programmes are liked least and why ?

(5) How villagers feel about the importance or value of the programmes (as useful, needed information or as entertainment) ?

How to get at these aspects

Meet different kinds of people from your TV audience and put them to talk individually, of what they have seen. If you can draw people into a conversation it will be very useful. Another thing that can be done is to observe the behaviour of people minutely during the TV programme. Observe how attentively they view, what is the level of noise, who see and who do not see, but talk with their neighbours/friends. Also observe if people nod their heads approving/not approving a programme. Choose farmers as your sample for evaluating programme on agriculture or married couples for learning about their knowledge of family planning practices but for general approval/disapproval of family planning norms your sample will be from all walks of life—age/caste/status/etc. That is, you should enquire about the impact of a programme from the segment of the population, for whom the programme has been made.

How to write the report

(1) Describe audience character and size at different points of time i.e. in the beginning of the programme, during the programme and at the end of the programme. Do your best to give a dynamic picture. Also tell how many males, femals and children and if possible people, belonging to different castes and occupational group comprise the audience.

(2) Note down during the programme what happens to audience during the programme. They watch quietly with interest, talk among themselves, level of noise and source of noise (children, adults, women or any other specify).

(3) Observe if any remark is made about the salient aspects of the programmes with each other or whether people repeat the words uttered by the actors or read titles on the screen.

You have to keep your eyes and ears open and sensitize your mind to observe during and after the broadcast to appreciate the public reaction to the broadcast. You should also be careful to discuss only relevant points. For example, do not discuss agricultural hardcore programmes with non-agriculturists, or the question adoption of family planning practices with unmarried boys and girls, so on and so forth. Remember one thing : Talk to many people to get various shades of opinion. Satisfy yourself that you are not getting stereotyped answers or false answers given in the hope of pleasing you. Finally remember that in order to make your findings generalizable for the village you have to collect information from a wide variety of persons such as illiterate farmers, literate persons, agriculturists, and non-agriculturists. But your data collection differs from quantitative feedback. You discuss thoroughly with a small number of people and report.

(5) Also report if there are electricity failures or other things which affect TV viewing.

The list of the programmes to be broadcast between 16th December 1975 to 31st December 1975 is enclosed. You have to get feed-back for programmes which are ticked. Remember you have no schedule or questionnaire. The points suggested will be your interview guide. Every day observe and interview and mail your report to us. This is job is to bo done. However. your activities should not be affected.

APPENDIX-VII

DAILY OBSERVATION SHEET OF TV VIEWERS

Enclosed you will find copies of Daily TV Viewers Observation Sheet. This sheet has been prepared for recording the sitting and the viewing locations of the various *jatis,* religions, age, sex, etc. in your village. In case of morning programme the sitting positions of the various children should be marked. Kindly use this sheet every day when you are visiting the TV centre and record the data. Additional information based on your observations should be recorded on the back of the sheet. The data thus collected should be sent in original along with the weekly report.

Instructions

1. Form REC will be used only for daily observation. One sheet will be used for one day's programme (either morning or evening).
2. You must fill all the columns in the sheet.
3. On the back sheet, you must write the names of the programmes that you observed on that day.
4. All observations must be taken at 'mid point time' of the programme. In other words if your programme starts at 6.30 p.m. and goes on up to 7.30 p.m. you must make your observation at 6.55 p.m.
5. Kindly use △ for male, □ for female, and ○ children, where you can observe differences of sex you can draw squares on □ for female and △ for male.
6. Any person (both sexes) below age 12 is defined as child for our study.
7. On this sheet you can also indicate religious groups and jati groups. In case you do so, use colour pencils or use some method of notations for the purpose of analysis.
8. In each observation sheet you must locate the TV position and sitting position of the viewers.
9. Each cube represents 5 persons. In other words if you fill one cube you are essentially saying that there are five

viewers sitting on that location.

10. In actual operation you draw encircled △, ○, or □ in the cube which means that few persons are sitting there.
11. You have to be imaginative to fill the observation sheet. Try to fill the cubes in such a fashion that a casual observer of these sheets can get a clear picture.
12. In case there is only one person standing or sitting use one straight line in the circle for marking it.

Please follow the instructions carefully,

APPENDIX—VIII

OBJECTIVES OF STUDY

For last one year you have been doing field work (except those who joined late). During this period of field work efforts have been made to collect general data. Get fully absorbed in the village life, and observe how people reacted to television and its programmes. Now the time has come when we must address ourselves with more specific questions related to our objectives of study and special areas of investigation related to SITE which help in formulating policies and taking decisions.

VILLAGE AND LAND

Our main objective is to study the process of existing communication in a 'village' and to investigate changes being brought about due to introduction of TV communication. The first and foremost question is then what is a village which is our unit of observation ? In order to answer this question let us collect specific data. Procure all related maps of the revenue villages in which your 'TV settlement' falls. To be more precise guidelines below will certainly help you. From local record, (available either with *Patvari*, Land Record Inspector etc.) draw the 'revenue village/s' map/s along with the details of land distribution. For this purpose you will have to contact a number of local officials and spend few days in collecting the data. While doing so please collect the following details:

(a) Copy the actual revenue village maps (all those falling in 'TV Settlement').
(b) Enlist the names of those persons who own land in these revenue villages.
(c) Classify and record land quality and land holding (land

quality classification as followed in the map ?

(d) Collect detailed records of crops as described by the Agriculture Department (VLW may be the best person to give details of last year).

(e) Collect information about crop records as described by the Revenue Department of last five years.

(f) Mark the area in these maps about your investigation area and 'TV Settlement'.

Take as many details as you think needed.

VILLAGE AND OTHER FACILITIES

Post office

Where is it located ? For how many years is it existing ? What kind of facilities are provided ? (MO/Telegrams/Saving facilities). Are there more than one post office in the village ? Who runs the Post Office ? What has been the utility pattern of the Post Office? How many letters/parcels/money orders/telegrams, etc., are received or sent by the villagers ? What is the system of post delivery?

Try to collect the data for the last five years about the above activities. All figures should be accurately collected in quantitative terms. Use the classification as followed in the Post Office. In short, write a five years detailed case study of the Post Office and its interaction with the village and its utilization pattern.

School

Give full details of the school/schools (if more than one, then details of each school be given separately). Describe the location of the school in relation to the village, number of teachers in the school (sex wise /agewise) where do they live? Do they belong to village or come from outside ?

Organizational set up of the school—Is it a *private/government/panchayat* run school, etc. ? What is its source of funds ? Describe the *type of building*, number of rooms, location of TV, location of power connection (draw maps/charts as needed). Describe number of classes in the school. Collect data on attendance and enrolment of the students for last five years. Classification of students according to the villages they belong to? In other words, mention about each student in the context of the place of his/her residence and the name of the village from where he/she comes to school for study (collect this data from records about the names of enrolled students and actual attendance for last five years). And finally give details on drop outs (a drop out is a person who though enrolled in the school, has for one reason or other decided to discontinue the studies).

SPECIAL FEATURE ABOUT ATTENDANCE

Collect data separately from August 1, 1975 to October 31, 1976 on the enrolment figures and actual attendance of the students in the school. As well as on total enrolment and attendance figures about male/female students besides separate classwise data.

Collect data on the transfer of teachers in and from the school during the last five years. All major events related to the history of the school should be focused. Similarly collect data on the enrolment of the students for last five years (start from January/July 1971).

Electricity power

(a) Write in detail as to when and in what form the electricity was supplied to this village first and how was utilised., e.g. irrigation/domestic/both.
(b) Where is the electricity sub-station? From where is the electric power for this village made available?
(c) Details on staff and organization of the sub station. In case of electricity failures how the information is sent to sub-station/station, and how it is corrected ?

Sources : Full data as maintained by the station for the last five years regarding the arrival of electricity to the village of your study. About the information on frequent failures of electricity, approach the sub-station which maintain logbooks for this purpose. In case data is sent to higher office you have to go there.

Record electricity supply, (August 1, 1975-August 1, 1976.)

For this purpose you have to go back to your own data, as well as sub-station data, headquarters (Electricity Department) data. *Even though you find discrepancies in these data, do not change them nor point out to any one.*

DOCUMENTS

Please procure the following Documentary Records on Districts for Holistic Study.

1. Latest District Gazetteer
2. Census Hand Book of 1971/61
3. Geography book used in grade 3/4/5 of the district and published district plans in areas of :

   (a) Agriculture
   (b) Family Planning.
   (c) Health and Nutrition
   (d) And other special developmental activities
   (e) Any special material that highlights the district developmental activities.

4. Any other published material on the district and related material at the state level.

APPENDIX—IX

SUPPLEMENTARY DATA COLLECTION IN HOLISTIC STUDY VILLAGE

So far, in holistic study, we have been collecting qualitative data. It has given us some understanding of village communication pattern. Now, we want to supplement this data with some quantitative data and also hope to have some comparable data from other holistic study villages. For this purpose, we plan to use T1 study schedule.

Research Design

We will follow the following research design :

TABLE 1

Showing sampling distribution by sex, viewer/non-viewer

	Viewers	*Non-viewers*	*Total*
Male	30	30	60
Female	30	30	60
Total	60	60	120

For the purpose of this study, we will divide the village total adult population into two categories (a) adult viewers—those who view programme at least 4 times or more in a month (see question No. 56 of schedule) (b) adult non-viewers—those who do not view the programme or view them once in a month or not even that. An adult for this study is defined as one who is above the age of 15 years. After dividing the adults into viewers and non-viewers category, they will be further divided into male and famale categories. In this way, we will have four categories as shown in Table-1. From each category, selection of a random sample of 30 for the purpose of our study will be drawn.

Sampling

For sampling purposes, we will have to go to all the houses and ascertain the adult male/female population in terms of viewers and non-viewers. The data will be collected with the help of the 'House hold Census' which was used while census taking. After doing so, you will have to separate the population into 4 groups of sub population and then draw a random sample of 30 from each of the four sub-population groups. At this point, care must be taken in this direction that your respondents will not be substituted due to death or non-availability or migration etc. In case you are forced to substitute, you must keep a list of such 6 substitutes, beyond your normal sample of 30. The names of these substitutes should be enlisted below 30 names covered as per sample.

Instrument

The instrument is the same as the one like T1 study schedule. The major shift will be in the area of questioning. *PLEASE USE THIS INSTRUMENT AS A SCHEDULE GUIDE.* Ask all questions, and write full and detailed answers by the side of the questions (if possible verbatim). Your ability to get detailed data is *most important*. Remember you are *NOT* filling a schedule only.

Data collection and training

Data collection will be done under the supervision of the Associate Scientists. The Associate Scientists will give you necessary training. Please ask as many questions to the Associate Scientists, as you think are needed to be clarified. They will be the final judges in terms of the data collection and training in the field.

All instructions originally given for the purpose of Survey data collection must be followed in this study and should be obtained from Associate Scientists. In Q. No. 15 of the schedule *DO NOT READ CATEGORIES*. But evaluate the credibility question as an open ended question.

REFERENCES CITED

Agrawal, Binod C. (1977a) Media Research and Anthropology : Some Observations on SITE. In *Evaluating Educational Television and Radio*, (eds.) Tony Bates and John Robinson, pp. 285-287. Milton Keynes : The Open University Press.

Agrawal, Binod C. (1977b) Satellite Instructional Television Experiment : A Social Evaluation. In *Evaluating Educational Television and Radio*. (eds.) Tony Bates and John Robinson, pp. 122-125. Milton Keynes : The Open University Press.

Agrawal, Binod C. (1978) *Television Comes to Village : An Evaluation of SITE*. Bangalore : Indian Space Research Organization.

Alfian and Godwin Chu (1979) *Satellite Television in Indonesia* (ed.) Hawaii: East-West Communication Institute.

Elder, Joseph W. (1968) Caste and World View : The Application of Survey Research Methods. In *Structure and Change in Indian Society* (ed.). Milton Singer and Bernard S. Cohn, pp. 173-186. New York : Wenner Gren Foundation.

Foster, George M. (1969) *Applied Anthropology*. Boston : Little Brown and Company.

Harris, Marvin (1968) *The Rise of Anthropological Theory*. New York : Thomas & Crowell Company.

Hoebel, Adamson (1966) *Anthropology : The Study of Man*. New York: Mc-Graw Hill Book Co.

Mc Anany, Emile (1977) Theme 2 Methodology—Report. In *Evaluating Educational Television and Radio* (Eds.) Tony Bates and John Robinson, pp. 356-364. Milton Keynes : The Open University Press.

Olien, Michael D. (1978) *The Human Myth : An Introduction of Anthropology*. New York : Harper and Row Publishers.

Redfield, Robert (1960) *The Little Community*. Chicago : The University of Chicago Press.

Rudolph, Lloyd and Susanne H. Rudolph (1960) Opinion Survey in India. In *Reader in Public Opinion and Communication*, Bernard Berelson and Morris Janowitz (eds.) pp. 745-55. New York : Free Press (Second edition).

Sapir, Edward (1966) (1931) Communication. In *Reader in Public Opinion and Communication*, Bernard Berelson and Morris Janowitz (Eds.) ; pp. 162-166. New York. The Free Press (Second edition).

Schramm, Wilbur (1973) *Men, Message and Media*. New York : Harper and Row Publishers.

Wallace, Anthony F.C. (1970) *Culture and Personality* (Second edition) New York : Random House.

INDEX